NASA/SP–2002-4526

MEMOIRS OF AN AERONAUTICAL ENGINEER
Flight Testing at Ames Research Center: 1940–1970

by

Seth B. Anderson

A Joint Publication of

NASA History Office
Office of External Relations
NASA Headquarters
Washington, DC

and

Ames Research Center
Moffett Field, California

Monographs in Aerospace History Series #26
June 2002

Library of Congress Cataloging-in-Publication Data

Anderson, Seth B.
  Memoirs of an aeronautical engineer : flight testing at Ames Research Center, 1940–1970 / by Seth B. Anderson
     p. cm.—(NASA history series) (Monographs in aerospace history ; #26) (NASA SP ; 2002-4526)
  Includes bibliographical references and index.
  ISBN 978-1-78039-309-4
  1. Anderson, Seth B. 2. Aeronautical engineers—United States—Biography. 3. Aeronautics—Research—United States—History. 4. Ames Research Center—History. I. Title. II. Series. III. Monographs in aerospace history ; no. 26. IV. NASA SP ; 4526.

TL540.A495 A3 2002
629.13'9902—dc21
  [B]   2002029509

To my wife, Libby,
for sharing memories

Libby Anderson on wing of a Vultee BT-13 basic trainer that was used in an Ames Research Center test pilot school (April 1944).

These memoirs take the reader back to the time when flight research was the principal activity at Ames Research Center. That period was made unique and exciting by the many unknowns that accompanied the early and rapid expansion of aircraft development. Flight research played an important role in finding essential answers to crucial aircraft flight problems.

What has happened to explain the end of an era in which aircraft flight research, which once had top priority at Ames, no longer even exists? People have not lost interest in airplanes, judging from the very large turnout at the annual convention of the Experimental Aircraft Association in Oshkosh, Wisconsin. Have all the important flight research areas been examined in sufficient depth to provide useful and lasting benefits? Only time will tell.

— Seth Anderson
October, 2000
Ames Research Center

Foreword

The words of the prologue are those of our friend and mentor, Seth Anderson, who dedicated his professional life to flight research. Seth wanted to preserve his personal flight research experiences for the benefit of future generations of aeronautical engineers and pilots—experiences he accumulated over several decades as a practitioner of the art and as a first-line supervisor of a like-minded and dedicated group. He believed that his recollections of important and exciting aspects of the programs in which he participated—the reasons for undertaking them, the personalities and conflicting opinions involved in them, the obstacles overcome, the problems solved, and the key results they produced—would be of interest not only to the aviation community but to the multitudes of aviation enthusiasts who remain fascinated by the extraordinary history of the adventure of flight.

Seth worked over a period of several years to prepare this monograph—collecting information, drafting the text, and finding and selecting the historic photographs. He describes the beginnings of flight research as he knew it at Ames Research Center, recalls numerous World War II programs, relates his experiences with powered-lift aircraft, and concludes with his impressions of two international flight research efforts. His comprehensive collection of large-format photographs of the airplanes and people involved in the various flight activities related in the text constitutes a compelling part of his work.

These memoirs were completed as Seth's 60-year career at the NACA and NASA ended with his death in 2001. As individuals who worked with and for Seth and shared his enthusiasm for airplanes and flight, we commend his memoirs for their excellence of content and style. Reading them leaves you with the feeling that you have just left Seth's office after hearing his recounting of the important activities of the day and that, primed by his enthusiasm, you are ready for the adventures to come.

Ames Research Center
Moffett Field, California

Jack Franklin
Dallas Denery

TABLE OF CONTENTS

THE BEGINNING YEARS 1
   Site Selection 1
   Locating the Facilities 1
   Need for Flight Research 1
   Purpose 2
   The Heritage 2
   The Scope 2

BACKGROUND 3
   Career Shaping 3
   Making the Right Choice 3

FLIGHT RESEARCH FACILITIES AND RELATED EVENTS 5
   Ames Status in the Very Early Years 5
   Shadows of WW II 6
   Early Flight Research Programs 6
   Need to Determine Handling Qualities 7
   Helping the War Effort 7
   Utility Aircraft 8
   Start of the Right Stuff 8
   Taste of Desert Flight Testing 9
   A Dead-stick Landing on Sand 11
   An Unexpected Close Look at the Southern Pacific Railroad Tracks 11
   Measuring the Correct Airspeed 12
   Going the Speed Limit 13
   Orchard Tree Pruning the Hard Way 13
   Lighter-than-air Episode 14
   Testing WW II Aircraft 15
   A Popular War Bird 15
   North American B-25D 16
   Grumman FM-2 17
   General Motors P-75A 17
   Need for a Stronger Vertical Tail 18
   Diving Out of Control 18
   Further Efforts to Alleviate Diving Tendencies 19
   Aerodynamic Braking Using the Propeller 19

    Improving a New Navy Carrier Aircraft 20
    Search for Satisfactory Stall Characteristics 21
    Pitch Behavior Differences 22
    Solving Flight Stall Problems 22
    Creating Super Booms 22
    Taming the Boundary Layer 23
    Effect of Aircraft Size—The Large 24
    Effect of Aircraft Size—The Small 24
    Helping Improve Navy Aircraft 25
    Encounter With Free-Air Balloons 25
    A Hurried Look at Flying Qualities 25
    Reducing Landing Ground Roll 26
    Aid for Crosswind Takeoffs 27
    Flying Saucers Are for Real 27

SHORT TAKEOFF AND LANDING AIRCRAFT 29
    YC-134A 29
    C-130B 29
    Convair Model 48 30
    Boeing 367-80 30
    A Personal Evaluation of the First U.S. Jet Transport 31
    Vertical Takeoff and Landing (VTOL) Aircraft 31
    Curving the Slipstream for High Lift 33
    Tilting the Thrust Vector 33
    A Lift Fan System 34

MISCELLANEOUS AIRCRAFT PROGRAMS 37
    An Unusual Wing Planform 37
    Comparison of Engine Air Inlets 38
    Increased Lift with Boundary-Layer Control 38
        North American F-86 39
        North American F-100A 39
        Grumman F9F-4 40
        North American FJ-3 40
    Summary of BLC Use 40

INTERNATIONAL FLIGHT RESEARCH PROGRAMS 41
    Improving the Handling of a Japanese Seaplane 41
    A French Connection for STOL Aircraft 41

 Ach du Lieber Senkrechtstarter (VTOL Transport) 42
MY CLOSING DAYS OF FLIGHT RESEARCH 45
 The End of an Era 45
A PICTURE STORY OF EARLY AMES FLIGHT RESEARCH 47
GLOSSARY 157
INDEX 159
ABOUT THE AUTHOR 163
MONOGRAPHS IN AEROSPACE HISTORY 165

The Beginning Years

Site Selection

Had it not been for the efforts of Charles A. Lindbergh, a name associated with many exciting flight adventures, flight research may not have started at Moffett Field, California, over 60 years ago. Although the idea of another site for expanding National Advisory Committee for Aeronautics (NACA) research had gained popularity in the late 1930s, for political reasons, Congress had repeatedly turned down funding for a West Coast site. Fortunately, Lindbergh, who headed a special survey committee for the new site, had flown to California in a new Army Curtiss P-36 fighter to examine potential sites. Convinced of the suitability of a Bay Area location, he helped obtain approval for funding the site at the Naval Air Station at Moffett Field.

Flight research was a significant consideration in selecting the site for the new NACA facility. (NACA was the predecessor of the National Aeronautics and Space Administration–NASA.) Among many important criteria for the location were the following: (1) the station should be on an Army or Navy base (airfield); (2) the site should allow for the construction of a flying field that would be about 1 mile square and be in an area of low air-traffic density with moderate temperatures and good flying weather throughout most of the year; and (3) the site should be in an area that provided attractive living conditions, schools, etc., and, if possible, should be near a university of recognized standing.

An existing site, previously used for the USS Macon dirigible in Mountain View, California, satisfied these conditions ideally, particularly the environmental aspects. Also, the surrounding communities were eager to have an additional revenue base. As a result, 39 acres of private, prime land were sold to the government for a mere $20,000. The address for the new facility—to be known as Ames Aeronautical Laboratory—could have been Mountain View, but the name Sunnyvale offered a more pleasing impression and would be less likely to provoke opposition to a West Coast selection. After considerable effort by many influential advocates, funding was approved and construction of the Ames facilities started in December 1939.

Locating the Facilities

An important consideration in constructing the new laboratory was the location for the flight research hangar. The view of the USS Macon dirigible, which arrived in October 1933 shows docking facilities at Moffett Field (fig. 1, see footnote on page 2). The clear area north of the dirigible hangar would become available for Ames facilities in 1939.

The location of the partially constructed hangar (building N-210) is shown in the May 1940 aerial photos, one looking east (fig. 2) and the other west (fig. 3). Building N-210 was located near the north end of the USS Macon dirigible hangar, close to the existing runways. The hangar was completed in August 1940, and as the oldest remnant of Ames history holds many exciting memories.

Aircraft access to the runway at the Naval Air Station was provided from either end of the hangar building by means of an existing road (Bushnell St.) on the south side and a yet-to-be completed taxi strip (now Ames Road) on the north end. In either case, aircraft had to taxi across railroad tracks, one set of which was originally used for ground handling of the world's largest dirigible, the USS Macon. Another set of tracks served the Navy warehouse on the north end. I remember times when returning aircraft had to wait for freight cars to clear the taxiway.

Need for Flight Research

The rapid progress of aviation resulted from many technological innovations that required conducting two closely related and essential aspects of flight in order to gain acceptance: flight testing and flight

Naval Air Station Sunnyvale, California; outside main entrance looking east (Oct. 1933).

research. It is important to understand the difference between the two in order to properly appreciate the value of each. For example, *flight testing* can determine how fast an aircraft will go; *flight research* can answer questions such as why it won't go faster.

In many of the early (1919) NACA programs, aircraft flight-test results were used to complement wind-tunnel data. On the other hand, NACA's 1917 Charter stated the purpose of flight research as being "...to supervise and direct the scientific study of the *problems of flight* with a view to their practical solution." It was an accepted fact that understanding the reasons for the behavior of aircraft would receive high priority at Ames.

As expected, World War II initially dominated flight activities at Ames. A wide variety of Army and Navy aircraft, from fighters to bombers, were flown for the purpose of exposing problems and finding solutions that would make them safer and more effective in their military missions. An important aspect of this work involved handling-qualities evaluations, particularly when limitations in controllability were identified. In the ensuing years, flight research was conducted on over 150 aircraft types.

Purpose

Although the story of Ames development has been published by other authors, the flight research results they covered were sometimes incomplete or presented in too little detail to provide a proper understanding of and an appreciation for the true value of the flight phase of aeronautical research. My purpose here is to provide a more complete description of flight research programs and their results, based on my personal recollection of events, and on my firsthand participation in many of them. The text also serves to highlight the technical and educational aspects of research, which helped shape early Ames progress in aeronautics. By reflecting on the growth and advancement of aviation stimulated by Ames flight research, a clearer appreciation of and a renewed interest in flight research at the National Aeronautics and Space Administration (NASA) Centers might evolve.

The Heritage

Few people are aware of the significance of the heritage provided by Ames flight research. For example, in 1957 Ames developed and flight tested a thrust reverser system that is now used worldwide as a means of reducing the landing distance of jet-powered transport aircraft. The first aircraft in-flight simulator was pioneered at Ames, and the first flight use of vortex generators to control flow separation on aircraft wings originated at Ames. Specifications for flying qualities of military aircraft were developed in large part from the results of Ames flight research. In addition, Federal Aviation Administration (FAA) certification specifications for vertical and short takeoff and landing aircraft stemmed from criteria developed by Ames testing of V/STOL aircraft.

The Scope

In writing this story of Ames flight research, a decision was made to restrict its scope to the early days when research on "little things" made an essential contribution. In retrospect, the little things, collectively, are what create the memories of people and events and thus constitute history. Unless documented by those who experienced them firsthand, accounts of them become obscured and inaccurate and lost to time.

The scope of these memoirs includes a description of the reasons for starting flight research during the challenging times fostered by the events of WW II. The text presents results of a selection of flight research programs which are set down in chronological order. Anecdotes are included together with a light biographical touch in order to provide some sense of the reality of dealing with hazardous flight situations. "Behind the scene" events reflect human nature response to the unexpected. The text concludes shortly after the switch-over was made from NACA to NASA in 1958—and Ames Aeronautical Laboratory became Ames Research Center—when the advocacy of and funding for major flight research was curbed by space research priorities.

---

* The figures that are cited in text are located at the end of this document (pages 49 to 155) and constitute a pictorial review of the flight research programs that are discussed in the text.

Background

Career Shaping

Flight research had barely started at Ames when I entered the "hangar" (building N-210) on 7 July 1942 to join the Flight Research Section and start a career with an unknown future. But first, how and why come to Ames?

I was raised on the outskirts of a small town in Illinois close to a small airport which early on triggered a curiosity about airplanes. As a youngster, I would try to get as close as possible to the flightpaths of these aircraft even though warned that "they may drop oil on you." Building scale models of popular aircraft and rubber-band-powered aircraft was a neighborhood activity. By visiting the airport frequently, I learned which aircraft were best by talking to local pilots and aircraft mechanics.

My first serious effort to get involved with aviation occurred in 1938 just after graduating from junior college. Because employment opportunities in the 1930 depression period were bleak, I applied to the Army Air Corps to become a pilot. However, having only two years of college, my qualifications were inadequate. Alas, the aircraft flight part of my career would have to wait for more advantageous circumstances.

A friend of a neighbor who was vice president of engineering for United Airlines influenced me to go to Purdue University and work toward a degree in aeronautical engineering. Between my junior and senior years, I worked at the United Airlines maintenance depot in Cheyenne, Wyoming, where airline transport aircraft went through periodic overhaul. This unique opportunity to help overhaul transport aircraft served to establish a better understanding of airline aircraft safety requirements, information that would prove helpful later.

After graduating from Purdue in June 1941, work opportunities were plentiful at several aircraft companies. I chose the NACA Langley Aeronautical Laboratory in Hampton, Virginia, because of my interest in doing basic research. Although the work in the Flight Research Branch there was interesting, the weather was not. It was very hot and humid throughout the summer, and air conditioning was yet to be discovered in the tide-water regions of Virginia. Quite unhappy with the environment, I took advantage of an opportunity to go back to Purdue for a masters degree in a program that involved work on a NACA-sponsored flight research project involving propeller efficiency.

In looking for a job in June 1942, I made inquiries about employment at the newly established Ames Aeronautical Laboratory in air-conditioned California. Work prospects at Ames did not look promising, however; a personnel interviewer at NACA told me there were no openings at Ames and that Langley Laboratory needed people to conduct research on WW II aircraft flight problems.

Making the Right Choice

Armed with a strong belief that California was the promised land of opportunity, I arrived in Palo Alto, California, on 4 July 1942 to seek employment at the West Coast NACA Ames facility. Without any prior contact with Ames management, I approached the personnel office in building N-210 with considerable apprehension. Being asked if the required application forms had been submitted served only to increase my anxiety. After examining my curriculum vitae (which was above average), the young lady in charge of personnel smiled and asked, "Where in the Laboratory would you like to work?"

There were two flight-related options available—the Flight Engineering Branch, which was hardware oriented, and the Flight Research Branch, which involved basic research and flight testing similar to that I had experienced at Langley.

My choice of flight research was fortunate, because the next day the Flight Research Section head, who was an Ames test pilot, asked me to go along on a flight that involved testing a heat exchanger for anti-icing applications. Little did I know how this flight would influence my future endeavors: it showed that I had some inherent flying talent.

The aircraft was a three-place North American O-47A observation aircraft which had a complete set of dual controls in the rear cockpit. With a natural curiosity about aircraft handling qualities and some rudimentary instruction, performing flight maneuvers was easy and helped identify with the data plotted when I had worked at Langley. After about an hour of exploring the handling-qualities behavior of the O-47A, the pilot suggested that I set up a downwind leg over the Bayshore highway at an altitude of 1,500 feet. With further coaching on when to turn, the airplane was positioned on final approach at the correct airspeed and rate of descent to land at Moffett. At about 100 feet over Bayshore highway, I said to the pilot "take over"; he replied, "Continue on, you're doing fine." After a little more forceful persuasion, he landed the aircraft. Upon deplaning I profusely thanked the pilot for the opportunity to experience a taste of test flying. He then said "You did very well, you're a pilot aren't you"? I'll never forget the look on his face when I replied, "I've never flown an airplane before in my life."

Flight Research Facilities and Related Events

Ames Status in the Very Early Years

A 1940 view (fig. 4) shows the layout of the early Ames facilities. The Flight Research building (N-210) is in the immediate foreground with "NACA" painted on the roof for aerial recognition. My office was on the first floor at the far north end. Another view (fig. 5) taken slightly later gives a second perspective of the hangar location. A 1942 photo (fig. 6) taken from the top of the USS *Macon* hangar shows two Sikorsky OS2U-2 aircraft parked in front of the south hangar door of building N-210. Cars were parked on the hangar apron; no one locked car doors, even on weekends. The offices on the east side of the building were for flight research and flight engineering and also served as temporary quarters for all administrative functions, including the office of the engineer in charge, personnel, fiscal, and library. The only other research activity in the building had to do with theoretical aerodynamics.

There were about 300 people at Ames in mid-1942—all were civil service employees; there were no contractors. Ames had no cafeteria and few amenities; we ate breakfast and lunch in the Navy mess hall. Although the wartime menus were limited in variety, the quantity was more than ample. Hershey bars with almonds were available, but only to active-duty military personnel.

When I started work at Ames (7 July 1942), there were only five aircraft in the hangar. Three were used for icing research—a North American O-47A observation plane, a Consolidated XB-24F Liberator (a heavy bomber), and a modified Lockheed 12-A Electra transport. In addition, a Vought Sikorsky OS2U-2 and a Brewster F2A-3 Buffalo were being used in performance and handling-qualities studies.

The wide open spaces are emphasized in the March 1943 view (fig. 7) of a C-46A-5 Curtiss Commando military transport used for icing and limited handling-qualities studies. The wing and tail surfaces were heated by engine exhaust gases for anti-icing. An O-47A aircraft (fig. 8) parked on the unimproved apron on the south side of building N-210, was also used for icing systems research.

A tool crib and an aircraft instrumentation shop occupied the west side of the building. Overhead on the second floor was a loft used for aircraft parts storage and for makeshift offices. Far removed from supervisory personnel, this was a popular place for telling war stories.

Flight data recording instruments were a key part of early flight research. Measurements of airspeed, altitude, acceleration, and angular velocities were photographically recorded and the film developed on site. In many cases the flight-test engineer helped develop the records and, after visually inspecting the data, planned the next flight.

In addition to nominal engineering duties, the research engineer served as a technician and installed instrumentation and wiring in test aircraft to expedite the test program. For the first time at NACA Ames, women aircraft mechanics worked alongside their male counterparts to overhaul and maintain the test aircraft. They were very capable and skillful, and made significant contributions to the war effort. In multiplace aircraft, research engineers flew in the test aircraft in order to monitor and adjust instrumentation. In contrast to the postwar leisurely pace of flight testing, an average of only 3 months passed from aircraft arrival at Ames to completion of flight tests and return of the aircraft to operational use. In 3 years during WW II, Ames flight tested and published reports on 56 different types of aircraft.

There were 26 people in the Flight Research Branch in 1944 (fig. 9) including engineers, pilots, mathematicians, and a secretary. The people who transcribed the data from the film and computed the engineering units for analysis by the research engineer were an important element of the team.

An important item in preparing for flight testing was adjusting aircraft weight and balance. Shown on the scales in figure 10 is a Lockheed P-38F Lightning fighter used in handling-qualities studies. The Bell P-39 Airacobra was involved in load measurements, and a Bell P-63 Kingcobra, in aileron flutter tests. All three test programs were conducted simultaneously because of the urgency to return the aircraft to squadron use.

In April 1943 the hangar was crowded with an interesting variety of 10 aircraft. Figure 11 was used to help convince NACA headquarters of the need to approve funding for a second hangar (building N-211) (fig. 12) to provide space for larger aircraft. I remember "borrowing" a few aircraft from the Navy to help make the point.

Shadows of WW II

Not only did WW II dominate research activities at Ames Aeronautical Laboratory, it also dominated one's life style. Because it took a governmental priority to get a cross-country railroad ticket in 1942, I had hitchhiked to California from Illinois. The trip took awhile—the strictly enforced wartime national speed limit was 35 mph. Finding Ames and getting to work was in itself an exciting challenge. Because of the fear of a Japanese invasion on the West Coast, there were no street lights, blackout shades covered all windows, and there were no signs directing visitors to Moffett Field or Ames. In leaving the hangar building at night, one was usually greeted by the sound of a rifle bolt from a nearby sentry who was ready to defend the area.

This wartime anxiety prevailed even for research facilities. When the 16-foot wind tunnel was being checked out in the early 1940s, the tunnel acoustics produced an ominous deep rumble which could be heard for miles because of an atmospheric inversion layer that reflected the sound more strongly in the Bay Area. When the tunnel was first operated in the middle of the night with no other sound distraction, it sounded like an approaching fleet of Japanese bombers. Following air-raid defense plans, all major electrical-power-absorbing equipment, including the wind-tunnel motors, was turned off. When this was done that evening, the enemy air raid appeared to have been called off and the tunnel motors were restarted, thereby creating another air-raid panic drill. After several cycles of on-off operation, logic prevailed and the military guards called it a night, allowing full operation of the tunnel.

Crossing the four-lane Bayshore highway at commute time via Moffett Boulevard was like playing Russian roulette since there were no lights to regulate the traffic. However, there was no traffic congestion on Sundays; on a trip to San Francisco, you might meet one or two cars. This low traffic density was made possible by wartime gasoline and tire rationing which severely restricted pleasure trips. This stay-at-home environment made social life a more popular pastime at Ames. At least one knew most of the people, and branch parties and dances were well attended.

Finding transportation was not easy. Cars were not produced during WW II, and even to purchase a bicycle required a special government form stating that the use of the bike was essential for the war effort. I had the good fortune to ride to work in the trunk of a friend's coupe along with another passenger. Fortunately there were no stop signs on Middlefield Road from Palo Alto to Moffett Field, only artichoke fields. Since the trunk hood remained open during the trip, this seating arrangement included a continuous and generous supply of debilitating carbon monoxide.

Early Flight Research Programs

In marked contrast to today's situation, flight research played the lead role in research activities at Ames. The subject of the first research authorization assigned to Ames from NACA headquarters and of the first technical report published at Ames (Sept. 1941) was aircraft icing, using a North American O-47A aircraft (fig. 13). This aircraft was used also for the first Ames flying-qualities measurements (Dec. 1942); in addition, it provided a service test function for newly developed flight data recording instruments. The flight study included the effect of adding an auxiliary vertical fin, instrumented for icing research, on the wing (fig. 14). This surface, mounted vertically at the mid-semispan of the main wing, had no detrimental effect on lateral-directional handling qualities. This was the start of many Ames flight programs that involved structural modifications to aircraft.

The second aircraft tested early in 1941 was a Lockheed 12A Electra which had been modified by Lockheed for use in conducting icing research in detail (fig. 15). Engine exhaust pipes, running through the wings' leading edges, heated the wing skin to prevent the formation of ice. The aircraft was flown into the most severe known icing conditions in tests that proved the feasibility of the exhaust heat method. This icing project was unique in that this was the first time a NACA research program was taken into the proof-of-concept stage in order to help solve a major flight operational problem. The thermal ice prevention system won the 1947 Collier Trophy, an annual award commemorating the most important achievement in American aviation. The people in Ames' Flight Engineering Section had demonstrated the value of flight testing in achieving important results.

The Lockheed 12A served also as a multi-passenger transport for short-haul missions. A trip to Hollister, California, was made in June 1943 to observe carrier landing practice for Navy aircraft; it was part of a flight research program undertaken to define reasons for limiting the reduction in landing approach speeds. The approaches and landings were spectacular to watch because engine power was abruptly cut at an airspeed close to stall from an altitude of about 15 feet. The need for the gear to be structurally designed for vertical drop rates of 25 feet per second for carrier aircraft operation was dramatically demonstrated in these "bounce" sessions.

President Harry Truman presenting the Collier Trophy to Lewis Rodert in December, 1947, for deicing research.

The 12A aircraft entered the traffic pattern clear of the practice area on the downwind leg of the approach, and the pilot actuated the switch to lower the electrically operated landing gear, but to no avail. The gear remained in the up position. The pilot was flying a racetrack pattern at 1,500 feet while he read the emergency gear-lowering instructions; he added to the anxiety by inadvertently allowing the aircraft to stall with a mild roll-off departure. With help from eager passengers, the gear was lowered manually by giving a crank handle 40 turns. Because the reason for the malfunction could not be determined, the trip back to Moffett Field was made with the gear extended.

The next aircraft tested in early 1942 was a Douglas SBD-1 Dauntless Navy bomber (fig. 16) which was involved in a very thorough flight-test program (33 flights, 47 flight hours) to document its handling qualities. In general, stability and control characteristics were considered satisfactory except for stall behavior in a landing approach, for which there was no warning and during which the roll-off was violent. Elevator stick force gradients were measured in dive pullouts at 400 miles per hour (about 0.7 Mach) which produced the onset of Mach compressibility effects.

Need to Determine Handling Qualities

Aircraft handling qualities had always been of vital interest to the military and NACA, because good handling qualities were essential to the acceptance of an aircraft. An aircraft's response to the pilot's input should be predictable without unwanted excursions or uncontrollable behavior. Good handling qualities insure safe aircraft operation. In the 1930s, only pilot opinion was used to judge the merits of an aircraft. The entry of the United States into WW II stimulated the proliferation of new military aircraft that had more powerful engines and expanded performance envelopes, and that for safe operation required quantitative guidelines for design and evaluation. An important ingredient supplied by Ames flight tests was a sound data base from which to develop credible handling-qualities specifications.

Helping the War Effort

In the early days of WW II, the military needed quick answers to operational problems, and service aircraft showed up at Ames for testing with clocklike regularity. Because these aircraft were taken directly from squadron use, time was of the essence and research work continued through Saturdays (no extra pay) to ensure their prompt return.

One most notable aircraft tested and modified in mid-1944 at Ames was a North American P-51B-1-NA Mustang, perhaps the most famous and best of all World War II fighters (fig. 17). This aircraft was the pride and joy of the Army Air Force because of its ability to provide long-range escort service for U.S. bombers. Although maneuverability and handling were superb, the horizontal stabilizers of several aircraft had failed structurally in attempted slow aileron rolls. These failures occurred at a time when early Ames flight tests revealed that the aircraft had unsatisfactory directional characteristics, including a reversal of rudder force at large angles of sideslip. It was reasoned that in a high-speed rolling pullout, adverse aileron yaw could generate sufficient sideslip to inadvertently cause a snap roll and thus impose large enough stresses to cause horizontal tail failure.

The Materiel Command, U.S. Army Air Forces, requested that Ames improve the directional characteristics of the P-51 to reduce sideslip excursions in rolling maneuvers while retaining existing rudder force change with airspeed. The modifications were to be simple in order to facilitate alterations to aircraft in service. The aircraft was tested with nine modifications in 13 flight conditions in sequence so that the relative merit of each could be evaluated.

Addition of a dorsal fin, rudder trailing-edge bulges, and a rudder antiboost-tab ratio of 1-to-2 gave the best overall flight behavior (fig. 18). The dorsal fin eliminated rudder-force reversals in sideslips, and had a favorable effect on structural loads. These Ames modifications essentially eliminated horizontal tail failures in maneuvering flight and were a major factor contributing to the popularity and success of the P-51 Mustang.

As another example, the Brewster F2A-3 Buffalo aircraft (fig. 19), which was undergoing tests in late 1942, had to be returned to Navy service when it was less than halfway through the flight-test program. Although the flying qualities were rated satisfactory, mission performance was so poor that it was ranked as one of the world's 10 worst military aircraft. It was rumored that Japanese fighter pilots were always delighted to spot a Brewster because it meant a sure victory was close at hand.

Utility Aircraft

During WW II, several aircraft were used to support the operations of research vehicles. These aircraft were used to pick up service parts for research aircraft, to provide instrument flight training for test pilots, and to ferry pilots and engineers to flight-test sites. Included were a North American O-47A, a Fairchild 24, two Howard GH-3s, a North American AT-6, and two Vultee BT-13s.

One of the BT-13s was modified to provide flight-test measurements of handling qualities for an Ames test pilots' school. The pilots flew a test program, recorded the data, and analyzed the results. During measurements of sideslip characteristics, data showed that the vertical fin of the BT-13 stalled in full-rudder sideslips. This was an important discovery, because this aircraft was a basic trainer and many student pilots were killed in training because of stall accidents. A closer look showed that a violent roll-off could occur if the plane stalled with flaps down in landing approach. Addition of a dorsal fin improved directional stability and alleviated this problem (fig. 20).

Carrying out these utility functions produced a few good anecdotes. On one occasion during WW II, the O-47A was used to transport people from Moffett Field to Muroc, California. A Navy fighter pilot who had just recently returned from combat duty in the Pacific was the pilot-in-command in the front seat. I had acquired my commercial pilot's license in 1944 and was flying the aircraft from the rear seat. Just after crossing the Tehachapi mountain range summit, heavy turbulence was encountered and the aircraft was abruptly upset from wings-level flight. After what seemed like several minutes of violent pitch, yaw, and roll motions, a passenger down below looked up and asked, "Can't you fly this aircraft any smoother?" "I could if I can get this control stick back in its socket," I replied. The stick had come out of its base during the first hard negative "g" (g = acceleration due to gravity, about 32 feet per second^2) when I had instinctively held on to it to avoid hitting my head on the canopy. The battle-weary Navy pilot was of no help in this situation—he was sound asleep in the front cockpit.

Coming back to Moffett was also exciting. Because I had flown this route several times, the Navy pilot preferred to relax and enjoy the scenery. Everything was fine until we approached Gilroy, California, and found that low clouds typical of Bay Area weather required flight at lower than desired altitudes. I had chosen to fly directly over U.S. Route 101 when the Navy pilot said, "I'm lost, where are we?" I replied, "Turn left on the Bayshore highway—Moffett Field is about 3 minutes ahead." A normal landing was made to the relief of the passenger who long remembered my comment about highway navigation flying.

In another situation when flying the O-47A from Muroc to the Los Angeles area, there were several unusual incidents. While flying over the desert, which was for the most part quite desolate, a strange object unexpectedly came into view. Directly below was a realistic-looking battleship replica made up to resemble a Japanese warship. It was used to train pilots in making bombing runs. This brought further questions about my navigational abilities; no one believed I was on the right course when a battleship was spotted in the middle of the desert.

Flying over Long Beach Harbor was rewarding in that directly below was the 180-ton, eight-engine Hughes H-4 Hercules (the Spruce Goose), the world's largest flying boat; in November 1947, it was classified and not normally available for public view. This plywood covered aircraft appeared huge, with its 320-foot wingspan. We landed at the Hughes-owned airport which consisted of a 13,000-foot grass strip close to Culver City, California (a suburb of Los Angeles).

Start of the Right Stuff

Typical of these early flight research programs was the rapid pace of testing which usually did not allow time for improving aircraft deficiencies. In some cases this had an adverse effect on government-industry relationships. For example, in July 1943, tests were conducted

Smith J. DeFrance.

to measure the flying-qualities characteristics of the new Consolidated Vultee A-35A Vengeance attack dive bomber (fig. 21). This aircraft, powered by a Wright Cyclone 1,600-horsepower engine, had exhaust stacks on each side of the fuselage close to the cockpit, and they were extremely noisy. Noise-suppressant earplugs had yet to be invented so we used cotton to obtain some relief. The high carbon-monoxide content in the engine exhaust made the air so bad in the cockpit that 100% oxygen had to be used at engine start-up and at all times during flight.

With dive brakes open (fig. 22), it was possible to perform a vertical dive of the A-35A from 15,000 feet without exceeding the placarded 300 mph airspeed. The unusual sensation of diving straight down at 37,000 feet per minute and hanging by the shoulder straps for 20 seconds at zero g (i.e., weightless) was novel and exhilarating. Needless to say, sinus congestion could not be tolerated for this high-rate-of-descent maneuver in an unpressurized cockpit.

I wrote a report noting that the aircraft failed to meet current military flying-qualities standards in several areas. Shortly after an advanced copy of the report was forwarded to the aircraft manufacturer, the vice president of Vultee, who was also the project test pilot for the A-35A, appeared at Ames wanting to know how we could have possibly found any shortcomings in his aircraft, which he personally developed, flight tested, and expected to sell to the Army Air Force. I was summoned to the office of Smith J. DeFrance, engineer in charge, expecting to suffer both in job longevity and technical credibility. I reviewed the factual evidence of the deficiencies identified from the flight data which included low longitudinal static stability, undesirable lateral characteristics in sideslip, and poor stall warning. I explained how the aircraft could be improved with only minor modifications. In the end, both Smitty DeFrance and the Vultee test pilot were smiling. I returned to my office remembering that a good engineer must also be a diplomat.

Taste of Desert Flight Testing

Many people may not be aware that Ames was the first NACA organization to conduct flight tests at Muroc Dry Lake, California (now Edwards AFB), in the latter years of WW II. This was before the High Speed Flight Station (now Dryden Flight Research Center) was established in 1946. During the tests, we stayed overnight in run-down Army Air Force barracks. Because the wind blew strongly during the night, the floor was covered with miniature sand dunes by morning.

Two high-performance aircraft, the North American P-51B Mustang and the then "secret" Lockheed YP-80 Shooting Star were tested by Ames at Muroc to take advantage of the large unrestricted flight-test area and ample room for landing in the event of an emergency. As it turned out, the test area served its purpose well, but with mixed results.

The P-51B (fig. 23) was flown to correlate flight drag measurements with results from a 1/3-scale P-51 model tested in the Ames 16-foot wind tunnel. Because an unpowered model was used in the tunnel tests, the flight tests were conducted without a propeller to eliminate slip-stream drag. The propellerless P-51 was attached to a twin-engine Northrop P-61 Black Widow by means of two long tow cables (attached to the P-51 at the nose spinner) and towed to altitude (fig. 24). At 28,000 feet, the P-51 pilot would release the tow line and glide down, taking accelerometer readings along the way to obtain drag performance. The tests progressed well until the third flight in September 1944 when, for unknown reasons, the tow cable prematurely released from the P-61 soon after takeoff from the north runway at Muroc. The tow line

North Base at Muroc Army Air Field (aerial view circa 1940s).

snapped back and bent the P-51 airspeed boom causing the pilot's airspeed to read low. Because the aircraft's airspeed was too high, the pilot could not, in the distance available, make a turn back to the smooth part of the lake bed for landing. The aircraft was flown under a top power line, struck the intermediate line, landed off the lake bed and rolled into a gravel pit. The pilot walked away from the accident relatively unscathed. After being taken to the base hospital for x-rays, it was discovered there was no power for the x-ray machine because the power transmission line had been severed in the ill-fated landing approach. Fortunately, enough data from previous flights were available to establish a reasonable drag correlation. The P-51 was not severely damaged and was trucked back to Ames and repaired. The pilot however, chose to give up test flying shortly afterward.

Tests of the YP-80, the first pre-production U.S. jet-powered fighter in 1944, were equally exciting. This was early when engine flameouts and turbine disc failures were frequent. Armor plating was used in the fuselage to protect the cables to the elevator control. Shock-wave-induced flow separation occurred on the ailerons causing "aileron buzz," and a resonant flow in the engine intake caused "duct rumble."

The aircraft had been instrumented at Ames in a special secured "Blue Room" on the floor of building N-210 hangar in mid-1944. The "secret" airplane was pushed out of the south end of the hangar unannounced after working hours to start taxi runs (fig. 25). At this time only one flight research engineer had seen the airplane, which was flown to Muroc over a weekend.

The first test flights were made from the Muroc North Base flight-test facility to calibrate the airspeed system in mid-December 1944. It was important that an accurate airspeed system be used because flights were to be made over a yet unexplored speed and altitude range. A North American O-47A aircraft with a calibrated airspeed system was flown in formation as a pace aircraft in several flights at altitudes around 20,000 feet. I was fortunate to be the flight-test engineer and sat in the rear cockpit of the O-47A to coordinate the tests and record data. I will always remember first views of the sleek, novel-looking YP-80 fighter aircraft flying in close formation.

There was an unfortunate, unrelated fatal accident which involved operational testing of the Army Air Force YP-80 during the Ames flight-test period at

Muroc. A point of interest at the time was whether the glow of jet engine exhaust would be visible at night to another close-flying enemy aircraft. A camera-equipped B-25 medium bomber and the YP-80, both flown at 10,000 feet without navigation lights, got the answer—the hard way. I remember seeing the wreckage of the two aircraft on a flatbed truck. For some unexplained reason they had collided in mid-air over the test area.

A Dead-stick Landing on Sand

Early in 1945, after completing a series of check flights from Muroc North Base, the first handling-qualities evaluation flights of the YP-80 would again demonstrate the value of flight testing over a large dry-lake bed. At 35,000 feet, measurements were made to document a strange directional oscillation associated with an audible duct rumble that occurred in sideslip flight. During a large sideslip excursion, the engine flamed out and could not be restarted. The highly experienced test pilot expected "no problem" in making a power-off landing on the large dry-lake bed. However, because the engine-driven hydraulic pump was inoperative and hydraulic pressure was required to lower the landing gear, a hand-pump emergency system was used to extend the gear. Unfortunately, because of an ergonomics problem, the "easy" landing turned difficult. Because the pilot had to hold the hydraulic selector valve in the emergency position, actuate the hydraulic pump, and also fly the aircraft, it was not possible to develop enough hydraulic pressure to completely lock the gear in the down position. The gear folded during the roll-out on Rogers dry-lake bed causing moderate damage to this specially instrumented test aircraft.

The duct rumble problem was solved by adding a splitter plate in the engine inlet duct to prevent a resonant airflow crossover. In addition, boundary-layer scoops were placed at the leading edge of the engine air inlet to remove low-energy air and improve pressure recovery at the engine compressor face.

After it was repaired (1 year later), the YP-80 was used to help solve some of the mysteries of flight in the transonic speed range (about 0.8-1.2 Mach). Two phenomena limited operations at high transonic speeds of fighter aircraft in the mid-1940s: aileron "buzz," or flutter, and abrupt pitch changes in high-speed flight.

Pressure measurements taken on the wing showed that above Mach 0.82, shock-wave-induced flow separation decreased static pressure on the upper wing surface resulting in aileron up-float and aileron "buzz." The flow separation also resulted in a change in tail effectiveness, causing the aircraft to pitch-up in dive recovery. During these tests, the aircraft was flown to Mach 0.866, the highest speed for any aircraft in the world at that time. This speed record remained until broken by the Bell XS-1 aircraft, which flew supersonic in the fall of 1947.

In January 1946, a production series Lockheed P-80A was given to Ames for continued flight tests. This aircraft was instrumented for a variety of flight programs (fig. 26). At the request of the Air Materiel Command, Army Air Forces, it was used first to obtain quantitative measurements of flying qualities. In a related program, pitch longitudinal dynamic stability studies were made using a servo-driven elevator control system. For these tests, the vertical location of the center of gravity (c.g.) was needed. This was determined by weighing the aircraft in nose-up and nose-down positions using strain gages (fig. 27).

An Unexpected Close Look at the Southern Pacific Railroad Tracks

Although there were no fatal flight accidents during the WW II test period, there were several accidents and harrowing flight experiences. The following anecdote from one test sequence vividly illustrates the challenge and danger of research test flying in the early days. It is important to reflect on the lessons learned from this and other examples of exploring the limits of the flight envelope.

In September 1943 flight tests were made on a Martin B-26B-21 Marauder twin-engine medium bomber (fig. 28) to determine whether a 6-foot wingspan addition would improve engine-out safety. This documented test was very important, because, if successful, it would allow the return of these aircraft to squadron use. Experience had indicated that the aircraft had only marginal performance and safety because of unsatisfactory roll/yaw control when one engine lost power at low airspeeds after takeoff. Many crew members were lost in combat and at the training field in Tampa Bay, Florida. Its notorious engine-out safety record inspired the nickname "Widow Maker" and "One-a-Day-in-Tampa Bay."

I was the flight-test engineer and after takeoff stood in the cockpit in back of the pilots to coordinate test runs. We headed north from Moffett Field on a Saturday morning to begin flight tests of the B-26 to explore the "dangerous" one-engine-out, low-speed part of the flight envelope. A stratocumulus overcast limited our test ceiling to an uncomfortably low 7,000 feet. With flaps and gear down, the left engine was abruptly throttled to idle and, with the right engine delivering full takeoff power, airspeed was gradually reduced. Straight flight was maintained by use of 250 pounds of right-rudder force and full nose-right rudder trim tab. I called on the intercom that the data were recorded satisfactorily. After reaching the lowest controllable airspeed (105 mph), the pilot, endeavoring to resume straight flight, abruptly removed power from the right engine forgetting to return the rudder trim tab to neutral from full nose-right. As a consequence, the aircraft yawed violently to the right and then back to the left as the pilot realized his mistake and returned power to the right engine. Sometimes, both the pilot and copilot were attempting to regain straight flight with counteracting rudder and engine power inputs. The aircraft behaved like a carnival ride, rapidly losing altitude and departing toward an incipient spin. Speculation was rife whether control would be regained before we ran out of altitude. Preferring not to end my flying career just then, I clipped on an emergency chest pack parachute. Amid shouts from the cockpit to the effect "I've got it!" the flight control situation further deteriorated. Not certain that recovery was imminent and observing that the ground was getting closer, I headed for the escape hatch calling out to the pilots, "I'm getting out—the flight data records are still on." "Not until I give the orders, you don't," said the venerable copilot. Shortly after that the rudder trim tab was returned to neutral, the airspeed increased, and control was regained. I glanced at the altimeter—we were at about 2,000 feet and directly over the Southern Pacific railroad tracks in San Mateo, a view that still lingers in my memory.

The foregoing clearly illustrates the danger of exploring flight boundary limits. No doubt the highly experienced flight crew, perhaps the best in the nation at the time, saved the day. The severity of the departure from controlled flight might have been mitigated by a preflight rehearsal of the test plan. Oh yes, the flight data indicated that the wing modification would improve flight safety provided that sufficient margins in airspeed were observed for low-speed operation.

Measuring the Correct Airspeed

An important point in documenting flight-research test results is an accurate value for aircraft airspeed. In-flight static pressure is influenced by a blocking effect of the wing/fuselage, resulting in erroneous readings of the aircraft's airspeed system. There were two ways to obtain accurate reference static pressure. One was a trailing "bomb" which was suspended by a cable 100 feet below the aircraft and which measured static pressure in undisturbed air. On one occasion when calibrating the airspeed system of a Douglas A-20A Havoc aircraft, the cable broke while we were flying over the Livermore hills. Looking for the bomb while flying down the canyons at an altitude of 100 feet at 250 mph was spectacular but uneventful.

Because the trailing bomb static reference method was airspeed-limited, another method was used to determine static pressure error. This consisted of flying by a known reference altitude and comparing the static pressure measured in the aircraft with the barometric static pressure at the flyby altitude. In the early days when air-traffic density was light, aircraft were flown by the top of Hangar 1 (called the Macon hangar) at increasing values of indicated airspeed. A phototheodolite was used to correct altitude disparities.

Getting to the top of the hangar with the instrument in June 1944, was in itself a challenge—not for the timid or those with acrophobia. I remember carefully

Interior of Hangar One.

walking up a curved wooden stairway to the narrow catwalks and looking down 200 feet at several yellow B-26B aircraft parked on the concrete floor. The final ascent was made by climbing a 20-foot vertical steel ladder leading to a small trap door that opened on to the roof. The view of artichoke fields and orchard land surrounding the four-lane Bayshore highway was spectacular. The view inspired a more leisurely return down the "hazardous" ladder.

Going the Speed Limit

The Douglas A-20A Havoc twin-engine midwing attack bomber (fig. 29) was another of a series of short-period loan aircraft sent to Ames in April 1943 for flying-qualities documentation. In addition to the pilot, the aircraft provided space for a navigator in the nose. Although there was no copilot on this twin-engine airplane, the rear cockpit was equipped with a control stick, rudder pedals, and engine power controls sufficient to provide an emergency fly-home capability in the event the pilot was incapacitated.

I was fortunate to be the flight test engineer and had the opportunity to "fly" the aircraft from the rear cockpit between test runs. Although control forces were unfavorably large and forward visibility was quite limited, evaluations showed that the aircraft could be maneuvered to a safe landing from the rear cockpit.

The A-20A had received favorable comments from operating squadrons, particularly regarding its directional control with one engine inoperative. One anomaly that Ames' flight tests disclosed was a potentially dangerous situation that had to do with the accuracy of indicated airspeed. The pitot-static head was mounted on top of the vertical fin (fig. 29), and cockpit airspeed meter readings varied considerably with change in sideslip angle. Stalls with one-engine inoperative and the other engine delivering full takeoff power (large sideslip condition) resulted in an error of 40 mph in indicated airspeed, enough to lead to an inadvertent stall in the event of an engine failure after takeoff.

Two anecdotes associated with high-speed operation of this aircraft are included here to illustrate the hazards and lessons learned in the early days of test flying at high airspeeds. Airspeed measurements were obtained from a boom mounted ahead of the aircraft nose to minimize pressure-blockage errors. A free-swiveling vane system aligned the sensors with the airstream to improve accuracy. One of the problems sometimes encountered was boom vibration (oscillations) which tended to increase in amplitude at high airspeeds. To check the airspeed boom on the A-20A for vibration tendencies, and because the boom could not be seen from the pilot's position (fig. 30), I unbuckled my parachute and crawled forward from the rear cockpit and occupied the navigator seat to observe the boom through the clear acrylic in the nose of the aircraft. After several dives to speeds approaching 400 mph with rates of descent over 25,000 feet per minute, I noted the onset of unsteadiness in the free-swiveling vane system. Since there was no direct escape from the nose area, I quickly returned to the rear cockpit after the aircraft had returned to level flight and slipped into my parachute harness for the flight back to Moffett.

Just after crossing Bayshore highway in final approach to landing, one of the metal vanes on the swiveling airspeed head came off, broke the nose acrylic windscreen, and penetrated the forward nose compartment. This added source of cooling air could be felt in the rear cockpit. Sometimes good luck is essential to flight testing. Had the vane failure occurred while I was observing the airspeed boom in the 400-mph dives, these memoirs would not have been written.

A second incident related to safety of flight occurred during tests to determine static longitudinal stability in the dive configuration. Inconsistent results in the curve of elevator force versus airspeed were observed; they suggested a disturbance in flow similar to that caused by shock-wave-induced flow separation. It was noted that the unusual force characteristics became progressively worse during the course of the program.

In a preflight inspection, the crew chief happened to lift the elevator control surface by the trailing edge. From its outward appearance it looked normal, but he noted an unusual flexibility. A closer inspection showed that the ribs were cracked at the connection to the elevator trailing edge and that the fabric had torn loose from the ribs internally as a result of the loads imposed in the high-speed dives. It was fortunate that a catastrophic failure of the elevator did not occur during the high-speed dives when large nose-up elevator inputs were used for recovery. The need to very carefully examine control surfaces for defects was an important lesson learned.

Orchard Tree Pruning the Hard Way

During the latter periods of WW II, the Navy requested tests of a new aircraft, the Douglas XSB2D-1 (fig. 31), which was powered by a new model Wright R-3350 air-cooled piston engine, the largest and most powerful engine (2,300 horsepower) ever developed to that time. Being large and heavy for a single-engine vehicle, it required a special propeller using advanced-technology cusped trailing-edge blades to improve performance. Navy operational trials showed the aircraft could not be precisely controlled in carrier approaches and wave-offs. Immediate help to identify potential solutions for the problem was needed.

The complete aircraft was tested in the large-scale 40- by 80-foot wind tunnel at Ames in July 1944, including full-power engine operation. A mechanic in the cockpit operated the engine (not a currently acceptable safety procedure). Because no answer for the unsatisfactory stability and control characteristics could be found in the tunnel tests, the aircraft was turned over to Ames flight research so the effects of flight dynamics could be included in studying the problem.

The flight-test part of the program had barely started in January 1946 when a forced landing ended the program prematurely. In climbing out from Moffett Field at about 4,000 feet, the engine began to surge in power and the aircraft was turned back for a precautionary landing. Shortly afterward, power was lost completely and it was obvious that a landing short of the runway was imminent. The test pilot selected a prune orchard clear of houses as the only possible landing site. Lining up between two tree rows with flaps down and gear up, the pilot skillfully hacked his way though 84 trees of the orchard that had previously been reserved for fruit pickers (fig. 32.) The aircraft came to a sudden stop resulting in a back injury to the project engineer in the rear cockpit. During the descent the engineer had the foresight to notify Moffett tower of the impending crash. It turned out that the orchard belonged to a good friend of the pilot; the pilot graciously declined to charge the farmer for his tree pruning efforts.

Pruning the orchard with the Douglas XSB2D-1.

Lighter-Than-Air Episode

One of the most unusual and certainly less known flight research programs conducted at Ames was carried out on a K-21 airship during April-October 1945. Nonrigid airships (blimps) had been used for submarine patrol missions along western U.S. shores by the Navy Fleet Airships Pacific. It was picturesque to look down from the air on a long line of these moored vehicles nodding into the wind along the seacoast highway from Pacifica to Santa Cruz (in Northern California) during the latter part of WW II. These missions were ideally suited to airships because of their extended in-flight and loiter capabilities.

By the same token, these long flights caused excessive pilot fatigue because of the poor handling qualities of the airships. In particular, pilot effort needed to move the controls was too great, and precision of flight-path control needed to be improved. Maneuverability was sluggish about all axes. For example, in a maximum effort dive pull-out maneuver with an instrumented vehicle, only 1.05 g's were recorded.

The Bureau of Aeronautics asked NACA to evaluate the handling qualities of a K-21 airship (fig. 33), which had been modified with aircraft-type control columns in place of the usual (separate) elevator and rudder control wheels. The purpose of the flight tests was to identify and quantify the causes of the poor handling qualities of the airship so that designers could incorporate improved mechanical control characteristics in future designs.

As would be expected, more than one flight-test engineer wanted the blimp duty. One day the project engineer for the blimp tests asked me to take his place on a 2:00 p.m. flight because he had a painful toothache and was scheduled to see a Navy dentist. I was delighted and was in the process of being checked out on operation of the instrumentation when the Flight Research Branch chief found out and insisted that a toothache was no excuse to reassign duty status. Apparently the engineer in charge had strongly insisted that only one person was cleared for the blimp duty, regardless of the circumstances.

Standard NACA photographic recording instruments were used in a 16-hour flight evaluation program. The results showed that the column control forces were uncomfortably large because of high control friction (25 pounds) and high inertia inherent in the control system. It was recommended that spring tabs be used to lower control forces and that friction and inertia be reduced to more closely compare with those of aircraft systems.

As part of my self-assigned duties in the blimp test program, it was fascinating to watch the ground handling of these unwieldy creatures of the sky. One stormy day in March 1945, I looked out of my office window in the south end of building N-210 to observe a K-ship (the largest of the series) being escorted into the north-end of Hangar 1 by the blimp ground crew. This close-up view of the docking operation was unusual, because normally the airships were hangared from the south end to take advantage of the prevailing northerly winds. I noted that because of the strong winds, several additional ground crew members were being added to guide the ship through the open hangar doors. The K-ship was halfway through the hangar

The K-21 Airship.

entrance when a strong updraft abruptly raised the tail. Noting that Mother Nature appeared to be getting the upper hand, and not wanting to go up with the ship, some of the Navy crew started to drop the mooring lines, much to the chagrin of those who felt honor-bound to stay with the ship. This quickly accelerated the upward motion of the tail-end of the ship. The envelope caught on the sharp edge of the hangar ceiling and a large hole was torn in the fabric. The blimp sagged like a sick whale on the concrete apron as the helium gas slowly escaped. Although there were no fatalities, several of the ground crew were injured in the free fall.

Testing WW II Aircraft

Wartime flight testing of aircraft was recognized as hazardous and the flight crews wore seat-pack-type parachutes which fitted in a specially rounded seat pan. Ames pilots were very cautious and conservative in operation of the aircraft and flew within established airspeed and g limits. This was an important safety consideration for all the usual reasons, but also because loss of an aircraft early on would have seriously jeopardized future Ames flight research.

A Popular War Bird

The Boeing B-17 Flying Fortress, famous for its performance in bombing enemy targets in Europe, had an unsure beginning. The prototype (Boeing model 299) crashed on takeoff on its first flight because the flight controls were locked. The XB-17F model arrived at Ames in August 1942 for special modifications that would greatly improve its wartime mission capability (fig. 34). This four-engine aircraft had the potential for long-range bombing missions, and it was essential that its utility not be compromised by having to avoid flying in icing conditions. The Army Air Force was aware of Ames' work on the Lockheed 12A deicing system, and in late 1941 asked NACA to develop a system for the XB B-17. A safer system than that developed for the 12A aircraft was needed such that the wing skin of the bomber would not be exposed to the hot engine exhaust gas in the event that the exhaust ducting was penetrated in combat. A heat exchanger system was developed and successfully demonstrated in severe icing conditions.

This modification was a good example of early Ames ingenuity and expertise and was recognized as a significant achievement by the military. NACA Ames flight research had provided a complete and satisfactory solution to a major military operational problem.

The XB-17F (fig. 35) served another important flight-research function in helping define handling-qualities criteria for large (bomber) aircraft. Tests were conducted in a short period from September 1942 to January 1943 (20 flight hours) at the request of the

The Boeing XB-17F with turbocharged engines (1942).

U.S. Army Air Force. Since this type aircraft was operated in long-duration missions, good handling qualities were highly desirable as a means of helping to minimize pilot fatigue and of improving gunner accuracy in combat missions.

I was the flight-test engineer and was positioned behind the pilots in a seat normally occupied by the radio operator. The opportunity to observe cockpit operations and view the outside world from all positions—from those of the tail gunner in the rear and the bombardier in the nose—was interesting, particularly during takeoff and landing. If necessary to move through the bomb bay in flight, one's parachute had to be removed. I enjoyed operating the gun turrets and "shooting down enemy aircraft."

I had the good fortune to occasionally act as copilot on these B-17 flights. On my first flight, starting engines 1, 2, and 3 was no problem, but the starter for number 4 would not engage. Alas, my dream to be part of a wartime flight crew team seemed doomed. Thanks to the aircraft crew chief, however, who manually engaged the starter from the ground, we taxied out for the test flight.

Several deficiencies were identified which could affect flight safety at low airspeeds. In particular, pitch stability was unsatisfactory below trim speed for all flight conditions, causing airspeed to diverge from a selected value and requiring constant pilot attention. In addition, roll-control power was inadequate with the flaps and gear down.

Stall characteristics were rated very unsatisfactory in power approach and go-around because of the lack of stall warning and an abrupt roll departure from wings-level. This occurred because the propeller slipstream suppressed airflow separation on the inboard portion of the wing, allowing stall to occur near the wing tips which caused a roll tendency. Because of unknown effects of flow asymmetries, no stalls were conducted with power off on an outboard engine.

On one flight, stall tests were conducted at 8,000 feet at the south end of the Santa Clara Valley. From the copilot's seat, the sudden 90-degree roll-off in the stall with this large aircraft was a thrilling experience and provided a unique view of the small town of Saratoga, California, directly below.

One scenario, which was commonplace with this type aircraft during WW II involved stall characteristics. Flaps and gear were down in preparation for landing at an austere field. Because of an obstruction on the field, a go-around was necessary. Maximum engine power was applied and the aircraft nose was raised to achieve maximum climb performance. Suddenly, without warning, the aircraft stalled and rolled violently to the left to a bank angle of about 90 degrees at 85 mph with an immediate large loss of altitude. This large departure from controlled flight would probably have been catastrophic for a fatigued pilot returning from a grueling combat mission.

North American B-25D

The B-25D Mitchell medium bomber, made famous by the April 1942 Doolittle raid over Tokyo, was a twin-engine, mid-wing bomber which came to Ames in March 1943 for flying-qualities studies (fig. 36). The research program was conducted at the request of the Materiel Command, U.S. Army Air Forces. Of special interest were directional stability and control characteristics. The handling qualities were rated satisfactory except for a reduction in directional stability at large sideslip angles. The Ames test results showed that by limiting maximum rudder travel and reducing rudder boost tab ratio, handling qualities were greatly improved.

These tests were not without incident. On one occasion, the female instrument coordinator in the Branch asked to go along on a flight which involved tests to measure the control force gradient in pull-up/push-down maneuvers. Apparently she neglected to fasten her seat belt securely, because in one of the more vigorous push-down tests, she floated upward and was plastered to the top of the cockpit cabin for several seconds. Fortunately, she was not injured, but this satisfied her curiosity about test flying and she did not volunteer to go on any subsequent flights.

Standard photographic recording instruments were used to measure control positions and forces. Calibration of the elevator control force system was made by locking the control surface in neutral and applying various forces to the control wheel using a large "fish scale" weighing device. In one instance the flight-test engineer knelt down and sighted along the top of the scale to ensure that the forces were applied perpendicularly to the control column. While applying maximum pull force, the hook slipped off the control wheel and the sharp edge of the scale struck the flight-test engineer at the bridge of his nose. This produced a permanent dent and left him with the nickname "No Nose" Kauffman.

In tests made to determine elevator control power in takeoff, measurements were being made of the ability to raise the nose wheel from the ground at a specific forward airspeed for several c.g. positions. During one of these tests, the pilot positioned the elevator control full nose-up, added takeoff power and started to roll forward. When the propeller slipstream reached the horizontal tail, the aircraft abruptly pitched up to where the fuselage tail contacted the ground and the aircraft remained in a full nose-high position. The aircraft crew chief came over as the venerable test pilot opened the cockpit window and called down, "I think we have the center of gravity too far aft."

Grumman FM-2
The Grumman FM-2 was a U.S. Navy fighter built by the Eastern Aircraft Division of the General Motors Corporation (fig. 37). It came to Ames in March 1945 for general flying-qualities tests. The FM-2 was powered by a Wright R-1820-56 engine; it was flown extensively in the Pacific as a light escort carrier fighter, and had established a favorable reputation with carrier pilots.

Flight tests had just started with the instrumented aircraft when a new pilot fresh out of the Pacific war theater joined Ames to become a test pilot. He had flown the FM-2 in combat and was lavish in praise of its fighting capability. He was assigned to conduct the flight-test program, although he had only meager flight-test experience. He came back from his first short flight in the test aircraft with a puzzled look. Everyone was anxious to know if he still liked the FM-2. He replied that the performance was similar to what he remembered, but he asked the flight-test engineer to take out the spring that was put in the aileron control system. Since no one had modified the aircraft, the pilot was accused of poor memory.

Out of curiosity though, I climbed into the cockpit and found that for certain stick positions the lateral control would move back to neutral by itself when released, as if it were spring loaded. All the inspection panels on the wing were removed and a close look showed what had happened. Apparently when taxiing out, a bolt had slipped out of the aileron control connection to the aileron bell crank, and the torque tube which moved the ailerons was wedged in a way to apply torsional resistance when the control stick was displaced from neutral. The bolt was replaced and the flight program completed without further incident thereby vindicating the combat veteran pilot.

General Motors P-75A
The P-75A (fig. 38) came to Ames in November 1944 for a special handling-qualities evaluation. The design was unique in that it used parts from other fighter aircraft to reduce design, labor, and structural material costs. The wing outer panels and the horizontal stabilizer were from a Curtiss P-40 fighter. Two Allison engines similar to those used in the P-40 were located behind the pilot and connected in tandem to two three-bladed counterrotating propellers driven by a long driveshaft to the propeller gear box.

The aircraft had several handling-qualities deficiencies and mediocre performance, and it was plagued by numerous mechanical problems. One day after a test flight, it taxied in with smoke coming from the rear engine. The pilot scrambled out of the cockpit on a dead run, and the fire was quickly extinguished by the ground crew.

Shortly after this incident, it was decided that a fire alarm box should be located close to the ramp where the aircraft were parked. One was placed at the intersection of the walkway from building N-210 and the aircraft apron. It was only about 2 feet high (to avoid its being hit by an aircraft wing).

One day a 5-year old boy wandered down the walkway, saw the bright red alarm box and, being curious about what would happen, pulled down the lever on the box. He was rewarded by what every youngster dreams about. Two large red fire engines drove up with sirens wailing. Although no harm was done, it was embarrassing to the father who was one of the country's leading test pilots and had an impeccable reputation for always doing things right. A memo to staff reminded all that no unescorted people were allowed on the ramp.

Need for a Stronger Vertical Tail

Aerodynamic loads were measured on the Bell P-39 Airacobra in an effort to understand its unusual out-of-control maneuvering behavior. The P-39 (fig. 39) was a single-engine, single-place aircraft with a rich military history. The muzzle of a 37-mm canon extended through the propeller spinner. Access to the small cockpit was by an unusual car-door-type entrance and was designed for pilots not over 5 feet 8 inches tall. The Allison liquid-cooled V-12 engine located in back of the pilot was connected to a propeller gearbox by means of an enclosed driveshaft between the pilot's legs. The driveshaft ran at engine speed and made an annoying noise.

The P-39 without a turbocharger had relatively poor performance at altitude, and some handling-qualities problems further compromised its operational utility. In particular, stall behavior and warning were unsatisfactory. There was no buffet to warn of an impending stall, and the aircraft departed in a snap roll if sideslip or yaw rate was not held to zero in turning on final approach. In high-speed flight, compressibility effects started at 0.62 Mach; however, the aircraft could be flown to Mach 0.80 and still recover using normal elevator control. The stick-force gradient in maneuvers was unusually low, about 2 pounds per g, making it easy to stall with little pilot effort. In squadron use it had a notorious reputation for inadvertent entry into a flat spin.

In the fall of 1944, I attended a meeting in which a young Army Air Force captain asked for NACA Ames help in identifying the cause of the unusual maneuvering behavior of this fighter. He pointed out that when stalled in a high-g turn, the aircraft sometimes appeared to tumble, end over end, out of control, as if the horizontal tail had lost effectiveness. Subsequently, a P-39 was instrumented at Ames to measure aerodynamic pressures on the aircraft when it was flown to the extremes of the flight envelope. The results indicated that when maneuvered at high speeds, the effectiveness of the horizontal tail remained normal. Measurements of loads on the vertical tail showed that during a high-speed rolling pull-out maneuver, sufficient sideslip could develop to exceed design side-load limits.

Other flight tests showed that the vertical tail was the culprit related to the tumble problem. Bell Aircraft Co. studies showed that in some extreme maneuvers structural failure of the vertical tail did occur in such a manner as to dislodge the horizontal tail—mystery solved. A stronger vertical fin spar was then added to all P-39 fighters.

Diving Out of Control

Reducing the diving tendency of high-performance fighters was an important research effort during WW II. Most fighter aircraft experienced a strong nose-down trim change at high transonic airspeeds which was created by a shock-wave-induced airflow separation on the wing. One popular aircraft, the Lockheed P-38J-15 Lightning (fig. 40), had serious operational problems in dives (discussed later). The P-38F model shown on the scales during a weight and balance check in building N-210 (fig. 10) was of special interest in Ames tests of stability and control. These flight tests were comprehensive, including evaluations at forward, mid, and rear c.g. locations, low and high altitude (30,000 feet), and the effect of external fuel tanks.

In general for the tests conducted, the aircraft's handling impressed pilots favorably, there being only mild deterioration noted at high altitude *provided* that the Mach number was less than 0.65 (about 400 mph). At higher speeds, transonic flow compressibility effects resulted in serious dive-recovery control problems. In operational squadron flights at Mach 0.74, flow separation on the wings caused the aircraft to vibrate and buck severely. The control column flailed back and forth sharply enough to snatch the control wheel out of the pilot's hands.

As a curious young engineer, I asked why Ames pilots were not allowed to explore the higher-speed part of the flight envelope to determine the cause of and find a possible solution for the serious control problems. Although not officially disclosed, it was rumored that the chief designer of the aircraft did not want the NACA to publicly disclose the serious high-speed deficiencies of this aircraft. Consequently, Ames flight-test airspeeds were limited by edict from the engineer-in-charge to 0.65 Mach to downplay the control problem caused by compressibility effects. This was unfortunate because as discussed later, stability and control was an area in which Ames expertise excelled.

In reality, squadron operation indicated that in dives of the P-38 to about 0.67 Mach, shock-wave-induced flow separation started to occur on the inboard wing upper surface resulting in an increase in angle of attack over the horizontal tail. This caused the severe diving tendency. As speed increased to 0.74 Mach, the diving moment exceeded the ability of the horizontal tail to effect a recovery. This dive behavior seriously restricted operational use of the P-38 in combat. Other contemporary fighters, for example, the P-39 or the P-47, which had thinner wing sections, could penetrate the transonic flow region with less serious recovery problems.

The Ames 16-Foot High Speed Wind Tunnel.

The Army Air Forces asked both Langley and Ames to find an acceptable solution for this difficult problem. Model tests in the Ames 16-foot high-speed wind tunnel suggested a quick and easy fix by adding flaps on the lower surface of the wing at 33% chord to offset the loss in lift caused by shock-induced flow separation. This partially helped the problem. Again, Ames was not permitted to flight test this recommendation because Lockheed wanted full credit for improving a basic design deficiency. Flight tests showed that if the flaps were extended *before* diving, the aircraft could recover from angles of dive up to 45 degrees. Without flap extension, the maximum dive angle was limited to 15 degrees to avoid penetrating the severe compressibility region.

In summary, political considerations sometimes dominated Ames flight research contributions. The company team of aircraft designers did not foresee that using a 16%-thick airfoil section in proximity to a bulbous fuselage canopy and large engine nacelle would exacerbate flow separation that could not be eliminated without a major aircraft redesign.

Further Efforts to Alleviate Diving Tendencies

The problem of obtaining satisfactory pitch control at supercritical speeds continued to be an impediment to further speed increases in the 1940s. Contrary to the popular belief that some WW II fighters exceeded the speed of sound in full-power vertical dives, Ames tests indicated that the maximum Mach number obtainable in dive tests of high-performance WW II aircraft using calibrated airspeed systems was about 0.81. Reaching higher speeds was not possible because of the strong shock-wave drag associated with the relatively thick airfoil sections used on these fighters.

Wind-tunnel and flight data had established that the cause of the diving tendencies resulted from shock-induced airflow separation on the upper wing surface that produced an adverse change in tail angle of attack as the Mach number increased in the transonic region. Wind-tunnel tests also indicated that the diving tendency might be alleviated when the trailing-edge flaps were deflected upward a small amount.

To determine if beneficial effects were realizable in actual flight, two propeller-equipped fighter aircraft, one a North American P-51 (fig. 41) with an NACA 66.2-15.5 series airfoil and a Grumman F-8F (fig. 42) with a NACA 23018 series wing airfoil section, were flight tested in late 1947 with wing trailing-edge flaps deflected upward. The results indicated that on both aircraft the deflected flaps had the desired effect of reducing the variation of the horizontal tail angle of attack with Mach number. However, for the P-51, only a modest decrease in the diving tendency at high Mach number was obtained, and for the F-8F, there was no appreciable improvement in the diving tendency. Reflexing the flaps was not investigated or incorporated on other WW II aircraft for subsequent operational use.

Aerodynamic Braking Using the Propeller

A popular WW II fighter tested at Ames in late 1944 was the Republic P-47 Thunderbolt. Included were the P-47N-1, P-47D-25, and the XP47M. These aircraft were powered by Pratt and Whitney R-2800 engines and used Curtiss Electric controllable-pitch propellers.

Shown in figure 43 is the flight-test engineer who is checking the P-47 in preparation for handling-qualities tests and for use of the propeller in speed control during dives.

Limited routine flying-qualities tests were conducted at Ames on the N and M models of the P-47 over a flight envelope that precluded flying at high transonic speeds. Military operational use of the P-47 included dives to 500 miles per hour (indicated airspeed) (about 0.82 Mach), well into transonic airflow regions. Company-developed dive-recovery flaps aided recovery to level flight.

Use of the propeller for speed control was also of interest. This was studied using the P-47D-25 model which had wide-chord "paddle" propeller blades and a specially modified blade-pitch control system that if desired, allowed the blades to go to reverse pitch for in-flight speed limiting. This airplane had been flown by the Army Air Forces at Wright Field for system checkout and was given to NACA Ames for the purpose of obtaining quantitative values of dive characteristics when using reversed propeller pitch in flight. Engine speed (rpm) was selected by a lever on the throttle quadrant which controlled propeller blade angle. In the event of a malfunction, an emergency switch button was provided to override the normal electric system.

About six flights were made over the Ames Mount Hamilton (Calif.) test area with reversed propeller pitch. Those tests indicated that airspeed could be controlled to placarded values in vertical dives. The wake from the propeller resulted in only a mild increase in buffet and unsteady flight behavior.

In the next test sequence to terminal velocity, the pilot noted that when the propeller pitch-control lever was moved out of the reverse position to obtain forward thrust, engine rpm increased beyond normal limits. This indicated that there had been a failure in the rpm governing system. To correct this problem, the aircraft was pulled out of the dive to a level flight attitude, and repeated efforts were made to obtain forward thrust. Normal changes in throttle and propeller pitch control were not successful. Next, the emergency button was depressed to override the electric governing system, but to no avail. The rate of sink was too high to consider a landing so the pilot detached the canopy in preparation to bail out (no ejection seat available). Just as the pilot was deciding where to leave the aircraft, electric contact in the pitch-control system was mysteriously restored. The pilot contacted Moffett tower and a normal, but breezy landing was made.

The foregoing is an example of a backup emergency system that was inadequate. Again "Lady Luck" seemed to provide a successful conclusion for what could have been a less fortunate episode in the story of the early days of flight research.

Improving a New Navy Carrier Aircraft

In 1943 the Ryan Aircraft Co. designed the FR-1 Fireball, a single-place carrier-based aircraft that would provide increased performance and engine-out safety. This new fighter featured a unique dual power plant consisting of a Wright R-1820 piston engine driving a three-blade tractor propeller and an additional GE turbojet engine with 1,600 pounds static thrust. Although high-speed performance of the combined power plants was not outstanding (425 mph), the value of the jet engine was demonstrated in a successful carrier landing with an unserviceable piston engine.

The turbine also had an additional use, although one of questionable value. The unit was mounted completely within the fuselage of the FR-1 aft of the pilot's compartment with the exhaust at the rear of the fuselage (fig. 44). Because this added and concealed source of forward thrust was not apparent to the casual observer, it was a source of amusement for Ames pilots. They would fly the FR-1 in formation with an another aircraft in the Bay Area and feather the propeller of the main (piston) engine. Much to the amazement of the pilot of the other aircraft, the Ryan aircraft did not lose altitude or position but continued to coast by in level flight using the unseen turbojet.

In late 1945, the Navy Bureau of Aeronautics asked Ames to conduct flight tests in an effort to improve the lateral stability of the Ryan FR-1 which exhibited negative lateral stability in carrier approaches. To find a cure for the lateral stability deficiency, large-scale 40- by 80-foot wind tunnel tests were run; they indicated that more wing geometric dihedral was needed—but how much? This was a question requiring a flight-research solution because of the dynamics involved. Too much dihedral would result in the aircraft being too sensitive in roll due to yawing. To resolve this question, three different FR-1s were company-modified to incorporate 7.5, 9.5, and 11.5 degrees of dihedral (fig. 45). The three aircraft were flown in rapid succession by several pilots to obtain a credible evaluation.

Because aircraft structural changes such as this are usually costly and time-consuming, another approach was desirable. One day looking at these aircraft parked on the ramp wing-tip to wing-tip, an engineer commented "There must be a better way"*

Grumman F6F-3

Lockheed F-104

ric dihedral for the internationally used high-performance F-104 Starfighter supersonic fighter.

Later, variable stability and control equipment was installed in North American's F-86 and F-100 swept-wing fighters to extend investigations to supersonic speeds where control tasks may change.

The lesson to be noted: sometimes a brute force approach can be the stimulus that leads to a valuable research method.

Search for Satisfactory Stall Characteristics

Stall/spin accidents have plagued the development of virtually all types of aircraft. Even today, they account for more fatal and serious injuries than any other kind of accident. The onset of the stall can be insidious, the pilot not expecting it and also being out of practice in making a safe stall recovery. Moreover, the stall usually occurs at too low an altitude to permit effective recovery.

As noted earlier, research of a basic nature had low priority during the war years except in those areas related to aircraft safety. An example was the need to establish a quantitative design criterion regarding stall warning. In order to provide a basis for quantitative evaluation, flight data from stalls of 16 airplanes ranging from single-engine fighters to four-engine bombers were examined in the 1940s to determine the quantitative factors related to pilot opinion of stall warning.

(to find the correct dihedral). At that moment the idea of using a variable-stability aircraft was born.

A short time later, servo-driven hardware for varying the effective dihedral in flight was assembled in the loft of building N-211 away from the prying eyes of the flight division chief who was not sympathetic to this ad hoc approach to flight research. The apparatus was installed in a surplus Grumman F6F-1 fighter (fig. 46) and over the years became the Nation's leading flight-research tool for solving lateral handling-qualities issues. Over 40 pilots flew the aircraft in various programs; the most notable of those programs was one undertaken to establish the correct (negative) geomet-

It was found in flight tests at Ames that stall warning was considered satisfactory when (1) airplane buffeting occurred at speeds from 3 to 15 mph above the stall speed with an increment of 0.04 to 0.22 g's, (2) preliminary controllable rolling motion from 0.04 to 0.06 radians per second occurred in a speed range from 2 to 12 mph above stall speed, and (3) rearward movement of the control stick of at least 2.75 inches took place immediately preceding the stall. These stall-warning criteria obtained from Ames flight tests are a valuable design tool used worldwide. Since they have not changed appreciably over the years, the results were fundamentally accurate.

Pitch Behavior Differences

Understanding the reasons for certain flight behavior is important for safety. As previously noted, a number of airplanes had experienced severe changes in stability and trim at transonic speeds.

I wrote reports documenting the high-speed flight characteristics of two popular fighters, the Lockheed P-80A (fig. 47) and the Republic P-84A (fig. 48). The P-80 exhibited a strong diving tendency starting at Mach 0.78, whereas the P-84A had a climbing tendency at the same airspeed.

Once again, my reports resulted in a request for my presence at the head office (in 1951) and once again there was some apprehension on my part. In the event, I met with the Ames engineer in charge and the chief engineer of the Republic Aircraft Co., who wanted to know why his WW II P-84A had an undesirable pitch trim change at high transonic speeds that was different from those of other contemporary fighters.

Of special interest in the discussion were data to show why two straight-wing jet fighters, although of generally similar configuration and with about the same wing thickness ratios, behaved differently at high transonic speeds. Understanding the causes was of interest to designers in that either of the tendencies shown by these two aircraft could limit the tactical high-speed operation and maneuverability of fighter aircraft.

The difference in the longitudinal behavior of the two airplanes was most noticeable to the pilot in unaccelerated flight and was confined to the lift coefficient range of 0.2 or less. Although the influence of factors affecting pitch behavior at high transonic Mach numbers was qualitatively understood, the magnitude and direction of the trim changes were difficult to predict because the result depended on a relatively small difference between two major inputs: a change in angle of attack at the horizontal tail and the wing pitching moment.

To help identify the causes for the pitch behavior differences, wing-section pressure distribution measurements had been made using flush-type orifices installed on the upper and lower wing surfaces at one spanwise location for both airplanes. An examination of the results in the transonic speed range indicated that a redistribution of lift caused by a more intense shock wave on the P-84 wing had the dominant effect of causing the undesirable climbing tendency, even though the tail experienced a nose-down trim change.

The flight data were convincing and the explanation was accepted as fact. The Republic chief engineer was not too happy, however, because he had personally selected the airfoil section used on the P-84A.

Solving Flight Stall Problems

Several high-speed aircraft using swept wings had poor stall behavior at high angles of attack because flow separation tended to occur initially at the wing tips, resulting in pitch instability and roll-off. High-lift devices such as leading-edge slats and leading-edge flaps delayed flow separation and improved stall behavior; however, these devices are mechanically complicated and heavy. Large-scale wind-tunnel tests of a swept-wing model with a cambered leading-edge wing showed large lift improvements comparable to those obtained with slats, but left some questions that required flight check. The uncertainties were (1) the effect on maximum lift and low-speed stalling characteristics, (2) high-speed longitudinal stability characteristics, and (3) drag changes at transonic speeds. Correlating wind-tunnel and flight results was a strong Ames asset.

Flight tests conducted in 1952 using a North American F-86A Sabre aircraft showed the versatility of flight research in obtaining quick answers to the foregoing questions. An example was tests of a mahogany leading edge shown under construction in the Ames sheet metal shop (fig. 49). The airfoil was contoured to provide increased camber, and the leading-edge radius was extended over the entire wing-span.

The airfoil was flown to 1.02 Mach with the following results. The modified leading edge provided lift coefficient increments 0.31 greater than that of the basic wing and 0.22 greater than with slats operating. The stalling characteristics, however, were unacceptable because of an abrupt roll-off and lack of stall warning. The addition of a short-chord fence (0.25 chord) at 0.63 semispan (fig. 50) improved the stall somewhat by restricting the outward flow of the boundary layer. Adding several fences (fig. 51) provided the best stall behavior (less roll-off), but at the sacrifice of low-speed performance. Flight tests up to 0.92 Mach confirmed that high-speed longitudinal stability and pitch trim were little affected by use of the modified leading edge. Finally, the drag of the modified aircraft was slightly higher in tests to a Mach number of 1.02.

Creating Super Booms

The nature of sonic booms caused by aircraft was not well understood in the early days of high-speed flight

North American F-86A

testing. During testing of modifications to North American swept-wing F-86s in the 1950s, the aircraft were dived from about 35,000 feet to obtain the highest possible Mach number (about 1.05). The test area assigned to Ames for flight tests was off the airways in the Mount Hamilton range over the Calaveras Reservoir region in California. Shortly after the flight-test program began, the local newspapers in the Pleasanton/Niles (California) area began reporting mysterious explosions which were strong enough to cause mild damage on the surface, but which could not be related to any local activity. It took some detective work to figure out that the explosions were caused by the shock waves emanating from the F-86 aircraft when it was flown at supersonic speeds. Ames was given credit, rightfully so, for making this phenomenon publicly known.

But there's more to the story. Although some connected with the F-86 flight-test program knew that sonic booms would be generated, no one appreciated that high-intensity booms (super booms) would occur because of the nature of the flightpath used in dive recovery. The curved flightpath appeared to focus the shock waves and produce larger overpressures compared with that created in level flight. This point was emphasized later that year when the Navy decided to open the Moffett air show with a sonic boom by flying their newly acquired swept-wing F9F-6 Cougars in a dive bombing maneuver at sonic speeds. I remember leaving building N-210 after work to witness a practice mission which turned out to be a lot better show than I expected. I was greeted by an earth shattering shock wave, generated by three aircraft, which broke dozens of windows at Moffett. Needless to say, this part of the air show was canceled.

Taming the Boundary Layer

Vortex generators (VGs)—protrusions on a wing surface designed to prevent the boundary layer from stalling—were first used in wind-tunnel tests in the mid-1940s to suppress flow separation and improve wing maximum lift. These devices provided an intermixing of the retarded boundary layer near the surface with higher energy airflow above the surface. The first in-flight use of this flow-improvement mechanism was conducted at Ames on the Lockheed YP-80 fighter in 1946.

As previously noted, shock-wave-induced flow separation on the wing caused major control problems for WW II fighters in high-speed dives. When swept-wing aircraft first appeared in the early 1950s, adverse compressibility flow effects— buffeting, wing-dropping (roll-off), and pitch-up—were noted in level flight at high transonic speeds. To improve boundary-layer flow, vortex generators were added to the swept-wing F-86A fighter airplane (fig. 52). The study included various size VGs in a variety of locations and in combination with other flow-control

Vortex generators mounted on the wing of a North American YF-86D.

devices including wing fences and wing leading-edge discontinuities.

Flight-test results on the F-86A with VGs indicated that the wing-dropping tendency was alleviated appreciably above a Mach number of 0.92 when the VGs were placed at 35% chord. In addition, the longitudinal instability (pitch-up) was reduced at Mach numbers between 0.90 and 0.94. The drag penalty incurred was negligible when the devices were located at 35% wing chord, but appreciable when used at 15% chord.

Vortex generators have been used continuously over the years by the aircraft industry, including on the latest Boeing 777 transport. Although not invented by Ames, these first documented applications of VGs to high-performance aircraft stimulated interest and broadened their use worldwide. This is another example of a successful research spin-off that was spawned from NACA Ames flight research.

Effect of Aircraft Size—The Large

What effect should aircraft size have on loads and response design criteria? Prediction of the maneuvering tail loads in the early days was a problem, particularly for very large aircraft, because of the lack of experimental data to check against design criteria. In addition, the pilot's control feel might be affected by the inertia of the larger surfaces.

To help answer these questions, in the latter part of 1951 the Navy Bureau of Aeronautics made available a Lockheed Constitution, XR60-1, a double deck, 190-foot wingspan, four-engine transport for NACA flight tests (fig. 53). Unique for the time period was that all XR60-1 controls were hydraulically operated (no servo tabs). Although not large by today's standards, the tail height (50-feet) required cutting a special vertical entrance in the east end of the newly constructed Ames hangar (bldg. N-211).

The flight tests consisted of longitudinal, directional, and rolling pullout maneuvers carried out over a 2-week period. No handling-qualities or NACA pilot evaluations were made. Because of NACA's lack of experience in judging the consequences of excessive maneuvering loads, all flying was performed by Navy pilots regularly assigned to this type aircraft. For the first time, however, the NACA instrumentation provided quantitative measurements of maneuvering loads for a very large aircraft.

No unusual or unexpected results were disclosed. A noticeable time lag existed between the pilots' input and the aircraft response, and the aircraft reached higher g loads than desired. In yawing maneuvers, the largest vertical tail loads quite unexpectedly occurred when the pilot released the rudder pedal force during a sideslip. In part because of budgetary constraints, only two of these aircraft were built.

Effect of Aircraft Size—The Small

As previously noted, in studying handling-qualities requirements questions remained regarding the effect of aircraft size and weight on the pilot's judgment of response needs. One of the smallest vehicles flown at Ames was the Hiller YRO-1 Rotorcycle (fig. 54). This one-man helicopter, originally designed for the armed services for rescue and liaison purposes, was small and collapsible so that it could be parachuted to a "downed" pilot. Because of its simplicity, it could be assembled quickly for escape purposes. It was powered by a four-cylinder, two-cycle, 43-horsepower Nelson engine and had a gross weight of 500 pounds. Evaluations were made of its pitch, roll, and directional characteristics in hover close to the ground.

In general, the vehicle had very unsatisfactory control characteristics and would not have been suitable even for a quick, short hop back to friendly territory. Lateral control response was different for left and right control inputs and undesirable roll-pitch cross-coupling accompanied abrupt control inputs. Directional control was too sensitive in hover and was considered dangerous for general use. It was easy to lose all directional control to the left if rotor speed (rpm) was allowed to decay to a low value. Watching a skilled test pilot's attempt to touch down while the vehicle

The Hiller YRO-1 Rotorcycle (June 1963).

was still rotating to the right and drifting toward some parked vehicles was exciting and exemplified the operational limitations of the test vehicle. Because of its low utility value and poor handling characteristics, only a few Rotorcycles were built, and they were eventually given to U.S. museums.

Helping Improve Navy Aircraft

Handling-qualities studies were made at the request of the Navy Bureau of Aeronautics for the purpose of examining the control characteristics of the Vought-Sikorsky OS2U-2 Kingfisher single-engine aircraft (fig. 55). This popular aircraft was used in land and sea operations, and several versions of it were tested at Ames in 1942-1945. Of primary interest were its low-speed performance and flying qualities.

Tests were conducted on several versions including those with patented Maxwell leading-edge slots, various amounts of aileron droop, and a combination aileron-spoiler control system. The tests compared the relative merits of different methods for lateral control in approach and landing. In addition, the flight tests served to refine test techniques for studying low-speed lateral control systems. A patented (Zap) full-span flap system had been installed on one aircraft, but was not tested in its entirety because of a disagreement between the test pilot and the manufacturer regarding special remuneration for conducting the tests over the extremes of the flight envelope.

Improvements in pitch-control effectiveness were needed for the Kingfisher aircraft in order for it to be able to fly at low airspeeds when equipped with more effective trailing-edge flaps and for operating with a larger c.g. range. In this regard, flight tests were made of a double-hinged horizontal tail designed at Ames (fig. 56) which provided increased lift for a given tail size. The results indicated generally satisfactory flying characteristics. The tests verified that increased tail effectiveness could be obtained by this method; however, there were nonlinearities in elevator control forces with deflection. This study served its purpose, and double-hinged systems were used on other Navy aircraft.

This was the first time that an aerodynamic proof-of-concept control system was designed, constructed, and flight tested entirely by Ames personnel.

Encounter With Free-Air Balloons

It was noted above that the Navy used large helium-filled balloons for training in lighter-than-air operations. Some training was conducted in a tall building, large enough to house a full-size inflated balloon.

When returning from a test flight with the OS2U-2 aircraft in 1943, the control tower requested that we delay our landing because runway access was obstructed by a free-air-balloon race. Looking down from 1,500 feet I counted 10 silver-colored balloons poised for takeoff in a line across the runway. The start of the race was signaled by a Very pistol, and sand bags were released simultaneously from each crew basket. The lift-off was uneventful except for the balloon nearest the USS *Macon*'s hangar. Because of a moderate crosswind, the basket contacted the hangar several times during its ascent. Fortunately, the crew was able to remain in the basket. I should note that in the 1940s, wide open spaces were plentiful around Moffett Field.

This balloon-race activity was part of a movie sponsored by the Navy to highlight lighter-than-air flight. Actor Wallace Berry had the lead male role.

A Hurried Look at Flying Qualities

The quick pace of flight research during the last part of WW II is exemplified by tests of a Douglas XBT2D-1 Skyraider Navy aircraft (the prototype of the AD-1 Skyraider) powered by a Wright R-3350 2,300-horsepower radial engine (fig. 57). It first flew in March 1945, and was delivered to Ames and tested in the short period from 21–26 May 1945, which included the weekend. Only seven flights and 10 hours of flight time were completed. Ames had established a reputation for expediency and valuable pilot opinion. The aircraft stayed in production for 12 years.

The Skyraider was a carrier-based dive-bomber and torpedo carrier. A 2,000-pound torpedo was included in the flight tests (fig. 58) to determine if this large external store would influence the lateral-directional behavior of the aircraft.

The XBT2D-1 prototype had several deficiencies which were noted by the test pilot. Excessive pitch-control force gradient in turns and dive pullouts was one deficiency. Since the elevator boost tabs, which directly influence elevator control forces, had not been hooked up, the project engineer decided to implement a quick fix by using the tabs to lower the control forces. Ah, but what gearing to use? A gearing ratio selected from 7- by 10-foot wind tunnel model tests was tried, but unfortunately the flight tests disclosed serious oversensitivity control-force characteristics. This was an example of a "quick fix" proving unsatisfactory, much to the chagrin of the project engineer whose ego suffered adversely. Because test time was limited, an optimum gearing ratio could not be obtained.

The stall characteristics of the Skyraider, which were rated unsatisfactory because of an abrupt, large roll-off with no warning for all configurations, had to be improved. Although several potential "fixes" were available for flight testing, the Skyraider was recalled for immediate squadron test evaluation and the stall improvements would have to wait.

Reducing Landing Ground Roll

Passengers flying on today's jet transports are accustomed to the deceleration provided by engine thrust reversal after touchdown. Most are not aware that Ames flight research expedited the development of this braking technique.

The Ames reverser program dates back to the mid-1950s when a member of the Flight Research Branch requested approval to develop and flight test a thrust-reverser system for ground braking using a surplus Navy jet fighter. The Flight Division Office initially turned down requests for the program's approval, in part because of a lack of understanding of the value of the program and uncertainty about Ames' ability to design and construct this kind of system.

A short time later, a program was proposed to develop an *in-flight* thrust reverser with primary emphasis on its use for flightpath control, and as a speed brake for emergency descents. A Lockheed F-94C Starfire single-engine jet fighter (fig. 59) was modified to test a cylindrical, target-type, hydraulically actuated, fully controllable thrust reverser. It was completely designed, constructed, and flight tested at Ames in 1956. Ames' sheet metal shop reconstructed the rear of the Starfire's fuselage (fig. 60) to withstand the higher loads and skin temperatures imposed by the reverser system. I was the flight-test engineer and flew in the rear seat of the F-94C to coordinate and monitor data acquisition.

Flight tests indicated that improved flightpath control and large reductions in approach speed were realized when the reverser was used instead of the engine throttle for flightpath control in steep, low-power approaches. After touchdown, deceleration values of 0.3 g were obtained with full reverser thrust, resulting in reductions in landing rollout to about one-half that for wheel brakes alone.

A major aerodynamic flight deficiency of the Starfire was its strong nose-down pitch trim change when large values of reversed thrust were used for speed control. In addition, increases in skin temperature occurred on the blunt rear fuselage fairing, thus restricting use of full engine power, after landing, to speeds greater than 50 knots. The effect of overheating was brought to our attention when, while taxiing in one day, the crew chief noted smoke and a fire in the rear fuselage. The hot exhaust gases had burned a hole in the fuselage skin and caused a hydraulic line to rupture (fig. 61). Titanium fuselage skin eliminated that problem.

The successful results of the flight-research program quickly aroused the interest of the jet transport industry which appreciated the enhanced safety in landings; particularly on ice- or snow-covered runways. The Boeing Company came to Ames and examined the reverser in detail (figs. 62 and 63) for application to its 707 jet transport as an expeditious way to reduce ground rollout after landing. The Douglas Company was interested in using the device for in-flight speed control and for flightpath control in landing approach. It was incorporated for a short time on the engines of the Douglas DC-8 jet transports, but was discontinued after the consequences of inadvertent, asymmetric deployment in flight were examined. A thrust-reverser application was made also on a North American F-100 Super

In-flight thrust reversers on the Lockheed F-94C.

Sabre fighter. The system was tested in the Ames 40- by 80-Foot Wind Tunnel and in flight by USAF Wright Field personnel. Large pitch trim changes and reverser exhaust heating problems discouraged use of the reverser for fighter aircraft at that time.

A touch of favorable public relations for the reverser occurred as a result of the interest of a popular radio showman, Arthur Godfrey, who as an active pilot and strong supporter of NACA-developed technology, endorsed the safety aspects on national radio (fig. 64).

After completing the research phase of the reverser program, many pilots, military and civil, were given the opportunity to evaluate the system. This ended in November 1958 when a visiting pilot made a hard landing as a result of the nose-down trim change when increased reversed thrust was inadvertently used in flight close to the ground.

The reverser program is an excellent example of an early commercial technology spin-off for NACA. At the start, it was not fully appreciated that developing and testing the device would have such a strong effect on jet transport operation and that it would soon be used worldwide. In fact, its importance was clearly overlooked by NACA Headquarters in Washington, which originally turned down the job-order request because "This was too ambitious a program for Ames to undertake." An individual who later became the director of Lewis Research Center entered an ironic note in the margin of that letter: "Certainly NACA should not do anything ambitious."

In summary, this program made one of the more important contributions of Ames flight research. It also illustrates that the challenge of gaining acceptance to do research can be difficult, particularly when it involves an area with an unknown future. As it turned out, the air transport industry capitalized on the system's braking function and not on its use for in-flight speed or flightpath control, which by its nature had serious safety concerns.

Aid for Crosswind Takeoffs

Most people recognize that operating an aircraft in a crosswind may affect takeoff performance. The versatility of flight research at Ames was exemplified by a May 1949 program undertaken to study the effect of a 90-degree crosswind on the takeoff distance of a light (Piper Cub) airplane equipped with a crosswind landing gear (fig. 65). Tests were requested by the Civil Aeronautics Administration (CAA), the forerunner of the FAA, which was concerned about the safety aspects in calculating takeoff performance with an unorthodox gear.

The main wheels of this gear were free to caster through an angular range of 25 degrees in either direction (fig. 66), thus enabling the airplane to maintain a heading other than that of the direction of the ground run. In crosswind takeoffs, this feature allows the airplane to be at zero sideslip throughout the takeoff run. The airplane is pointed into the relative wind at progressively increasing angles with respect to the runway as aircraft speed increases. The purpose of this type of landing gear is to enable safer operation at airports having only a single runway.

The results showed that about 25% less ground run was required to attain takeoff speeds in a 16 mph 90-degree crosswind relative to calm wind conditions. Another interpretation of the results of interest to the CAA was that use of the crosswind gear would not compromise takeoff performance in normal operation regardless of wind direction. It was noted, however, that controlling direction when operating on a narrow taxi way with this gear was more of a sporting proposition in a strong crosswind. This feature was not incorporated on other aircraft to any great extent.

Flying Saucers Are for Real

In support of those firm believers who hold that extraterrestrial flying vehicles are disk-shaped and can hover, Ames was involved in wind-tunnel and flight tests of an 18-foot-diameter circular planform vertical takeoff and landing (VTOL) aircraft built by the Canadian Avro Aircraft firm in the 1960s. The VZ-9AV (fig. 67) had a design gross weight of 5,650 pounds and was first demonstrated with a pilot in early 1960. Although highly touted to be a superior weapon system for the Air Force and a flying tank for the Army, very serious stability, control, and propulsion system problems plagued efforts to develop the craft to an operational status.

Vertical lift was obtained from a 5-foot-diameter axial-flow fan mounted in the center of the disk, tip-turbine driven by the exhaust from three J-69 turbojet engines. The total exhaust was ejected downward around the circumference of the disk for vertical lift, and the efflux could be vectored aft for forward acceleration and also to provide roll, yaw, and pitch control (fig. 68). The jet sheet at the rear of the disk induced a large lift component calculated to be able to support the aircraft at a forward speed of 45 mph. Loss of propulsive power, however, would mean that the aircraft would not have control for a "glide" to a safe landing.

The VZ-9AV VTOL aircraft (Jan. 1963).

Full-scale 40- by 80-foot wind-tunnel tests made at Ames (fig. 69) in the early 1960s obtained aerodynamic force and moment data for the purpose of determining stability, control, and propulsion-system flow characteristics for transition and cruise flight. These tests indicated that the design had serious deficiencies that were far too complex to solve with state-of-the-art technology.

The VZ-9AV was flight tested to performance limits by an Ames pilot in Canada in 1960. Although unofficially predicted to be able to fly at 300 mph and 30,000 feet, it was shown that these performance estimates were off by several orders of magnitude—it barely attained 30 mph and an altitude of 3 feet. The low fan-thrust performance was caused by a thick boundary layer at the compressor inlet, stalling at the fan-blade tips, combined with large internal duct losses which greatly reduced lift, forward thrust, and control moments.

The design had a positive fountain effect (ground cushion) at low heights; however, above 3 feet the vehicle became dynamically unstable in pitch and roll with a motion aptly described as "hub capping." This was a result of a random separated flow on the under surface of the vehicle and reflected flow from the ground impinging upward on the vehicle. Substantial control cross-coupling and very large nose-up trim changes occurred with forward speed. Because there was no inherent directional stability and no directional damping, continuous control input and pilot effort were required to "fly" close to the ground.

In retrospect, the configuration was unquestionably ahead of its time. Certainly, it had inherent stealth features that would help defy radar detection. However, with three turbojets and a large high-speed fan, it could be heard long before being seen. The Ames pilot aptly described it as a 3,000-horsepower siren. Although appealing in an aesthetic sense, it had poor overall performance potential. The low-aspect-ratio, 20%-thickness-ratio disk had, at best, a cruise lift/drag (L/D) ratio of 3.5 compared with about 10 for most conventional-wing aircraft.

Although modern technology could improve the VZ-9AV's low-speed handling by using automatic control of vectored thrust, the large inherent trim changes and ground recirculation effects (hot-gas ingestion) would limit overall utility. In essence, it turned out to be a low-performance ground-effect machine capable of leaping over 10-foot ditches with comparative ease.

Short Takeoff and Landing Aircraft

Ames played a lead role in advancing the state of the art for short takeoff and landing (STOL) operation of transport aircraft through simulation and wind-tunnel and flight tests. Early STOL aircraft relied on low wing loading and conventional high-lift devices to reduce approach speed and obtain short landing distances. However, because landing approach required using idle power to descend, flightpath adjustment and touchdown accuracy were compromised.

Large-scale wind-tunnel tests had indicated that for propeller aircraft, large lift gains could be obtained by immersing the wing in the slipstream and using engine power (thrust) to augment aerodynamic lift. Questions remained, however, regarding how much of the powered-lift gains could be used to reduce approach speeds. Reduced stability, low control power and damping, which occurred at low airspeeds, could affect the pilot's ability to control flightpath in landing approach. Answers to these questions required flight research with aircraft capable of flying at very high lift coefficients. Some of the results are discussed next.

YC-134A

Initial powered-lift studies were made with a Stroukoff Corporation YC-134A, a two-engine transport built under Air Force contract in 1960 (fig. 70). For landing approach, the trailing-edge flaps were deflected 60 degrees and the ailerons drooped 30 degrees. Area suction boundary-layer control (BLC) was used to improve lift effectiveness at large surface deflections. A J-30 turbojet engine with a load compressor provided suction for the BLC systems.

The operating envelope for the YC-134A was enlarged appreciably in terms of stall-speed reduction by using the propeller slipstream to augment aerodynamic lift. However, in terms of flight-path angle and airspeed, obtaining desired STOL performance was limited because of the compromise imposed by the necessity of using engine power to obtain high lift and still achieve a desired sink rate for steep approaches. For the YC-134A, the difference in maximum lift between idle and 70% maximum power corresponded to a reduction of about 20 knots in stall speed. However, at only 0.3 (30%) maximum power, the effective lift-drag ratio was still too large to produce a flightpath angle much steeper than 4 degrees. Further landing-performance improvements would have required an increase in installed thrust-to-weight ratio and a more effective high-lift BLC system.

C-130B

A more advanced STOL transport, the Lockheed NC-130B (fig. 71), was thoroughly flight tested by Ames starting in 1962. For high lift, the trailing-edge flaps were deflected 90 degrees and the ailerons drooped 30 degrees. Airflow separation at these large surface deflections was minimized by a blowing-type BLC system which also provided air flow for improved rudder and elevator effectiveness. Two T-56 turboshaft engines driving load compressors mounted on outboard wing pods provided high pressure air for the BLC system.

The gains in landing performance were impressive. Compared with the standard C-130B, minimum approach speed was reduced from 106 knots to 63 knots and the landing distance was cut in half. Although only small gains in takeoff performance were possible in the STOL configuration, takeoff speeds were as low as 61 knots. To decrease takeoff distance, higher thrust-to-weight engines would be required. Wave-off or go-around capability was also unusual

The Lockheed NC-130B STOL turboprop-powered aircraft in front of the NASA hangar (Sept. 1961).

because of the marked nose-low pitch attitude needed in go-around at 85 knots with the flaps deflected 70 degrees (fig. 72). To produce a more positive climb angle, a reduction in flap deflection with an increase in stall-speed margin would be required.

Although the modified aircraft had good STOL performance, operational utility was compromised by unsatisfactory lateral-directional handling qualities. Low directional stability, low directional damping, and adverse yaw produced by lateral control deflection were responsible for large sideslip excursions during maneuvers in landing approach. A stability augmentation system using a single-axis (rudder-drive) input was developed to provide turn coordination, yaw-rate damping, and sideslip-rate damping for satisfactory operation at approach speeds as low as 70 knots.

Convair Model 48

One of the last of a series of propeller-driven STOL aircraft tested was the COIN (for Counter Insurgency) airplane (fig. 73). This single-seat aircraft—Convair Model 48—had two propellers and double-hinged, single-slotted flaps to deflect the slipstream on the largely immersed wing. The aircraft was designed to a Marine Corps operating requirement that specified a takeoff and landing distance of 500 feet over a 50-foot obstacle. It was to operate in a jungle environment and be small, simple, and inexpensive. An additional requirement included "single-engine survivability." This was accomplished by using a "torque-equalizer," which reduced power on one engine automatically in the event the other failed, thereby allowing the pilot to hold wings level long enough to eject safely.

About 10 hours of flight tests were conducted on the Model 48 in mid-summer 1967. Most flights were made in the landing configuration, because that was the principal problem area for most STOL aircraft. Landings were made at 55 to 60 knots with a rate of descent of about 700 feet per minute. This was approximately 10 knots below the power-off stall speed. The permissible sink speed of 16 feet per second for the landing gear made possible no-flare landings. This provided a great reduction in landing distance and improvement in touchdown point accuracy over that of a full flare landing. The pilot maintained a constant approach attitude into ground contact, initiated reverse propeller pitch, and used brakes as required.

Although good low-speed performance for the COIN mission was demonstrated, no COIN-type aircraft went into production. Part of the reason was safety. If flown above the minimum single-engine control speed, in compliance with normal safety restrictions for twin-engine aircraft, it was no better than other small twins.

Boeing 367-80

An unusual, large jet transport aircraft with STOL performance capability was the Boeing 367-80 (707 prototype) tested in May 1965. There were two areas of interest for this aircraft: (1) methods for implementing noise-abatement landing approaches and (2) handling qualities in operation at high lift coefficients. The aircraft had been modified by the Boeing Company for these programs.

A reduction in noise in landing approach was obtained by flying various approach profiles with reduced engine power (fig. 74). Three types of approach profiles were evaluated: (1) two-segment with a high beam of 6.0 degrees and a low beam of 2.65 degrees, (2) a curved-beam with an initial angle of 6.0 degrees, and (3) decelerating types in which the speed decreases during approach.

A comprehensive piloted simulation was utilized to develop the systems and operational techniques. For these tests an additional slotted auxiliary flap had been added to provide direct lift control (DLC) to improve flare and touchdown accuracy. Initial flights showed that these approaches were more demanding of the pilot and that for airline-type operation they would require advanced displays and a guidance system for two-segment profiles, a modified flight director, and an autothrottle.

The flight tests showed that the pilots preferred the two-segment profile, which could be flown with the same precision as a conventional approach without a significant increase in pilot workload. A significant reduction in landing-approach noise (about 10 PNdB (perceived noise level decibels)) could be achieved by flying the steep two-segment approach profile.

In the second part of the program, operation at higher lift coefficients in landing approach were examined. The aircraft had been modified to provide shroud-type blowing over highly deflected flaps for increased lift by using bleed air from the four jet engines (fig. 75). This allowed the airplane to be flown at approach speeds in the range of 122-112 knots compared with the nominal 170-150-knot speeds usually used.

A program using the Ames moving-cab transport simulator had indicated that the lateral-directional characteristics deteriorated to an unsatisfactory level as airspeed was reduced. The higher dihedral effect, adverse yaw owing to roll rate, and low damping were responsible. An augmentation system with roll-rate and sideslip-rate inputs to the rudder and inputs from sideslip, yaw rate, and roll rate were needed to provide fully satisfactory handling qualities for low-speed approaches. Increased roll-response sensitivity was an important factor that improved pilot opinion of roll control.

The flight tests verified the simulator results. As previously noted, pilot opinion was strongly influenced by roll-response sensitivity as measured by roll angular acceleration for a given lateral control deflection. Increased control sensitivity upgraded pilot opinion of roll response to satisfactory, even with relatively low roll-control power. The pilots considered the response of 10 degrees after 1 second more than adequate for instrument-flight-rule (IFR) approaches with this large aircraft.

A Personal Evaluation of the First U.S. Jet Transport

There was an early association between Ames and the Boeing Company in 1955 during the time the 707 swept-wing jet transport was undergoing flight certification tests. Because of Ames' experience with flight tests of swept-wing fighter aircraft, I was one of a few Ames engineers invited to participate in discussions of potential problems with swept-wing transport designs during takeoff and landing. At a meeting held in Seattle, Washington, design criteria for setting performance margins for FAA certification of the new transport were reviewed.

Although Boeing had done its usual excellent job in design, Ames flight tests identified two potential problems. One problem was stalling of the wing in takeoff at rotation to maximum ground attitude. Tests of the F-86 swept-wing jet fighter examined this wing stalling problem in the early 1950s. The second problem was vertical tail stall caused by large sideslip excursions resulting from failure of an outboard engine on multi-engine aircraft. This was based on Ames tests of a large four-engine STOL aircraft. Boeing took these points into consideration, because the production 707 aircraft utilized a wing leading-edge Kruger flap for stall protection and a dorsal fin for increased directional stability at large sideslip angles.

Two of us, who were Ames flight-test engineers, were invited to fly in the first operational demonstration of the 707 jet transport on 26 September 1957. A Pan American crew, complete with stewardesses, was onboard for the flight from Seattle, Washington, to Wichita, Kansas. It was an exciting experience traveling first class in the first operational flight of the first U.S. commercial jet transport.

In 1957 not many airlines were willing to gamble on using this new type of aircraft for cross-country operation. United Airlines, for example, was hesitant because of the unknown reliability of the new jet engines. United was recovering from growing pains with the high-powered Wright R-3350 turbo-compound internal combustion engines used on its DC-7s.

At the time, no one predicted or appreciated the tremendous and far-reaching impact that jet-powered transport aircraft would have on the worldwide travel industry. There were two selling points that were not fully appreciated at that time: lack of vibration in the cabin and the ability to fly over bad weather. The vibration point was demonstrated during the inaugural flight when the Pan Am captain placed a silver dollar on edge on a table in the lounge. Another point of personal interest in that flight was the long distance required for landing rollout. The aircraft had no thrust reversers. (See Reducing Landing Ground Roll on page 26.)

Vertical Takeoff and Landing (VTOL) Aircraft

Early in 1960, Ames used the X-14, built by the Bell Aircraft Company with USAF funding, to advance the state of the art for jet-powered VTOL aircraft (fig. 76). The X-14 was a single-place, twin-engine deflected turbojet using Bristol Siddeley Viper engines with cascade thrust diverters. Compressor bleed air was ducted to reaction nozzles at extremities of the aircraft to provide attitude control for hover and low-speed flight.

Early evaluation flights (fig. 77) indicated that the X-14 had marginal vertical lift capability and low control power for adjusting attitude in hover. Ames pilots were able to successfully demonstrate a verti-circuit (vertical takeoff, transition to cruise, and vertical landing). Not so for everyone, however. An experienced test pilot from the United Kingdom was given the opportunity to gain hover experience in this relatively uncomplicated jet VTOL aircraft before starting flight tests of the more complex British P1127 Kestrel experimental fighter (later developed into the Harrier). His first flight was short. After liftoff to hover in the Ames taxi-ramp area, small lateral excursions developed which the pilot could not precisely control; he decided to land and reduced engine thrust. Unfortunately, this action reduced the lateral control power which was needed to correct a right-wing-low attitude. The landing gear strut collapsed in a skidding touchdown. The pilot stated that the accident occurred because it appeared that roll control deteriorated and that a larger area for hovering was needed.

In a second incident, an Italian Air Force captain had completed a verti-circuit, and started to taxi in. For some reason, he elected to make one more liftoff to hover, without remembering to turn on the bleed air needed for the reaction control nozzles. After liftoff, the aircraft uncontrollably drifted backward in a tail-low attitude and was damaged in landing—much to the chagrin of the pilot who was the elite of the Italian Air Force.

These examples pointed up the danger of allowing visiting pilots to hover a VTOL that had only marginal control power on a small taxi ramp. Subsequently, all visiting pilots "hovered" the aircraft at 1,500 feet after a conventional takeoff. The merit of this higher altitude test technique was demonstrated later by a Navy pilot who neglected to switch on the system for countering the engine gyroscopic moments. During a yawing maneuver, a strong pitch up occurred which resulted in the aircraft performing a loop at zero forward speed. About 500 feet of altitude was lost in recovering to stabilized flight.

Ames' X-14's flight research made valuable contributions to the design of future VTOLs. Perhaps the most significant of those contributions was the clarification of roll, pitch, and yaw control-power require-

X-14 in level flight at 4,000 ft.

ments. This included requirements for handling ground-effect disturbances, trim changes in transition flight, and maneuvering. The X-14A was also used to examine unique methods of control in hover and low-speed flight. One was the use of small tip-turbine-driven fans to augment lateral control force for improving roll angular acceleration. Another was a direct side-force lateral maneuvering system using a vane mounted in the engine exhaust (fig. 78). This device eliminated the necessity of rolling the aircraft to achieve a sideward thrust component for translation. Also documented were the requirements for dealing with engine gyroscopic cross-coupling (previously noted), aerodynamic suck-down, and the effects of hot-gas ingestion in hover operation.

The X-14 was also used to study soil erosion problems that might be encountered by turbojet VTOL aircraft operating from semi-prepared surfaces. In a brief flight investigation, the pilot made vertical descents over an open grass area to determine the height at which a disturbance of the underlying terrain would be apparent. At jet exhaust heights of 9 and 14 feet, held for 5 seconds, a slight browning of the grass sod was noticed. Following about 5 seconds of hover at 6 feet, the ground surface suddenly erupted with large chunks of soil and grass being hurled upward 8 to 10 feet (fig. 79). The resultant crater was about 6 feet in diameter and 6 inches deep. This debris was ingested into the engine intakes damaging the compressor blades and necessitating the replacement of both engines. This ad hoc type of flight testing was unique to the early days of flight research.

The aircraft was converted to a variable-stability and control configuration (X-14B) to provide increased research utility. One of the more notable examples of its versatility took place in 1965 when the aircraft was used to evaluate control and trajectory requirements for the Lunar Lander during final descent to landing on the Moon (fig. 80). The evaluation pilot was Neil Armstrong, who was the first man to step on the Moon; he flew a 1,000-foot vertical trajectory 1 mile from touchdown to land on a designated target. Of the four different flightpaths investigated, the pilot preferred the straight-line profile although it did use more fuel. While selecting control-power values for this task, the pilot required a view of both the horizon and the touchdown point.

The X-14 was used over a 20-year period, during which time several control improvements were made, including the installation of a digital variable-stability and control system. A hard landing in May 1981, caused by a control system malfunction, ended the X-14's career as a research vehicle. It was given to the Army museum at Fort Rucker, Alabama.

Curving the Slipstream for High Lift

Another aircraft designed for VTOL operation, which had a close developmental relationship with Ames, was the Ryan VZ-3RY (fig. 81). It had large-chord, double-slotted, highly deflected flaps and the deflected slipstream principal was used for high lift. It was powered by a single Lycoming YT-53 825-horsepower turboshaft engine which was geared to drive two wooden counterrotating propellers.

This aircraft, in spite of a rough start in early flight tests, was one of the more successful fixed-wing V/STOL designs. It arrived at Ames on 20 May 1958 and completed powered tests in the 40- by 80-foot wind tunnel in December 1958. It was first flown at Ames by a Ryan pilot in December 1958 and made 13 flights before being damaged in a high-sink-rate landing in February 1959.

After repairs were made by the Ryan Company, it returned to Ames in August 1959 and was transferred to Ames control in January 1960 to begin a flight-research program. A Ryan test pilot made some 19 flights to "fine tune" the vehicle for operation by other pilots. An Ames test pilot made four flights before a more serious accident occurred, one that warrants some discussion because it illustrates the unknown aspects of research flying in the early days.

The flying qualities, performance, and general limitations of this V/STOL design were investigated. Flights by a Ryan pilot and full-scale wind-tunnel data indicated that the aircraft had to be flown within established boundaries of airspeed, engine power, and angle of attack to avoid departure from controlled flight. Excessive airspeed could cause structural damage; too low an airspeed with insufficient thrust (slipstream velocity) could result in wing stall and reduction in pitch-control effectiveness.

In February 1960, an Ames test pilot made two flights at low flap settings as part of a checkout procedure to explore the low-speed flight envelope. On the third flight, the plan was to increase flap deflection to 70 degrees (maximum available) and to fly as slowly as possible. At 3,500 feet in level flight with 40 degrees of flaps and 80% engine rpm, full flaps were selected. The aircraft pitched up to an inverted position and departed from controlled flight. After various unsuccessful attempts to regain control, the test pilot ejected from the aircraft (he sustained a back injury during the ejection).

Because the aircraft had been previously flown with full flap by the Ryan pilot, an explanation of what went wrong in this early period of Ames flight research was needed. A review of the accident indicated that the primary mistake made by the Ames pilot was that he had not increased engine power as the flaps were lowered to maximum deflection. As a result, pitch-control power obtained by engine exhaust was less than adequate for nose-down trim, and the aerodynamic pitching moment (nose-down) associated with slipstream velocity was reduced resulting in a large nose-up out-of-trim condition. As far as was known, the Ryan chase pilot did not advise the Ames pilot to increase engine power when increasing flap deflection.

Since the VZ-3RY was a promising V/STOL research tool, it was rebuilt by the Ryan Company and flight tests were resumed in 1962. One of the first test programs investigated longitudinal (pitch) trim characteristics. No adverse effects were found over an airspeed range down to 24 knots; below 24 knots, however, wing stall occurred. Subsequent tests with the wing modified to incorporate leading-edge slats (fig. 82) showed that the aircraft could be flown to airspeeds down to 6 knots out of ground effect. Operation of the aircraft close to the ground (less than 15 feet) was limited because of loss of lift and reduced lateral control at airspeeds less than 20 knots; this was caused by recirculation of the propeller slipstream (fig. 83).

This program showed the benefits of combining piloted simulation, wind-tunnel tests, and flight tests in efforts to better understand the fundamental limitations of a particular lift design. This process was used to advantage in developing follow-on deflected slipstream vehicles including the Canadair CL-84, the Vought XC-142, and the Breguet 941 aircraft.

Tilting the Thrust Vector

The Bell Helicopter Company's XV-3 tilt-rotor concept (fig. 84) was unique in that it combined the rotor of a helicopter with the wing of an airplane to obtain VTOL operation. It is also another example of Ames taking a strong lead to find solutions to problems inherent in this VTOL concept. First flown in 1955, it was periodically tested in flight and in the 40- by 80-foot wind tunnel at Ames over an 11-year period.

Before coming to Ames, the vehicle had been flight tested at Edwards Air Force Base in a 30-hour program. Early tests indicated that the design was feasible with a

The Bell XV-3 experimental tilt rotor.

wide airspeed/angle-of-attack transition corridor, and that it could be flown through transition from conventional to rotorcraft flight with only minor trim changes (fig. 85). However, it had several design deficiencies which limited the operational envelope. First, it was underpowered (it could not hover out of ground effect), had poor cruise flight performance, and needed a more sophisticated control system to improve basic handling qualities. Second, evaluation flights showed that it could not be flown beyond 140 knots because of low-damped pitch and lateral-directional oscillations. This serious design deficiency was not identified in early wind-tunnel tests. Flight tests were required to show the destabilizing effect of the large chord, slow-turning rotors on aeroelastic and dynamic stability associated with high blade-flapping amplitude in airplane cruise mode (fig. 86).

The Ames flight-test program concentrated on obtaining a better understanding of the cause of the poor dynamic stability at high cruise speeds. It was determined that the principal part of the problem was caused by the large blade angles required for high-speed flight. If the rotors were located at the trailing edge of the wing (a pusher configuration), the in-plane normal force (aft of the c.g.) would be stabilizing. In addition, enlarging the area of the horizontal tail would extend the usable airspeed range.

Still to be resolved was an aeroelastic low-frequency rotor/pylon oscillation similar to a propeller whirl flutter mode in cruise flight. After an extensive analysis program aided by computer studies, the aircraft entered the 40- by 80-foot tunnel (in May 1966) for the fourth and last time. At maximum tunnel speed and at the last data point planned, a wing-tip-fatigue failure resulted in both rotors being torn off, thus ending the XV-3's test career.

A Lift Fan System

Another example of a V/STOL aircraft which received special development attention at Ames was the XV-5 fan-in-wing concept (fig. 87). In 1958 the General Electric Company introduced the idea of tip-driven lift fans for VTOL operation. The U.S. Army awarded a contract in 1961 to G.E. and the Ryan Company to build two demonstrator aircraft using the lift-fan concept. The Ryan XV-5, which first flew in July 1964, was a two-place, 0.8-Mach, twin-engine, mid-wing, research aircraft that had good hover characteristics and high-speed potential.

Two large, tip-driven lift fans (62 inches in diameter) were mounted in the wings, and a smaller third fan was mounted in the nose of the fuselage. The nose fan had a shutter-type closure above the fan and two doors below to modulate nose fan-lift for pitch control. Exhaust from two jet engines in the fuselage was diverted from conventional tailpipes to a common duct to provide thrust symmetry in case of an engine failure. "Butterfly" doors on the upper wing surface opened for hover and transition flight and closed for conventional flight. Spanwise louvers, which formed the lower skin surface, were open during VTOL operation. The fan exhaust could be vectored for transitional fore or aft acceleration, and, by a "pinching" action, spoiled lift thrust for height control. Yaw control was obtained by differential movement of the wing-fan exit louvers. Roll control was obtained by thrust modulation of wing-fan thrust, and pitch control by nose-fan and wing-fans.

In preparation for flight tests, a full-scale model of the XV-5A including the propulsive lift system was extensively tested in the Ames 40- by 80-Foot Wind Tunnel (fig. 88) and in an adjustable height ground rig (fig. 89) to optimize propulsive performance before flight. In addition, piloted simulation studies were made to examine the XV-5A's stability and control characteristics. In spite of this strong Ames role in developing the lift-fan concept, the early XV-5A aircraft was not flight tested at Ames; instead, it was evaluated in late 1966 at Edwards AFB. These evaluations by 15 test pilots demonstrated that the lift-fan concept had merit, and operational procedures appeared to be straightforward.

Not so, however, for lurking in the background was a conversion procedure that would result in a fatal accident.

Conversions between jet and fan flight modes had to be performed within a narrow airspeed corridor to maintain pitch attitude within safe limits. In converting to fan mode for VTOL operation, aircraft speed was reduced to about 95 knots, lift-fan doors were opened, and engine power increased. This resulted in a large nose-up pitch change, requiring a 10-degree nose-down stabilizer movement to maintain level flight.

There were two fatal accidents in demonstration flights of the XV-5A.

A conversion-related accident occurred during a press demonstration flight of the XV-5A at Edwards AFB in April 1965. During a high-speed low-altitude pass, the aircraft was observed to suddenly pitch down into a 45-degree dive from which it never recovered. The pilot ejected but at too low an altitude to survive. The accident board concluded that the pilot inadvertently actuated the conversion switch at too high an airspeed to maintain controlled flight. The aircraft was extensively damaged in the ensuing fire and was not repaired.

A second accident occurred in an XV-5A that had been rigged with a pilot-operated rescue hoist, located on the left side of the fuselage just ahead of the lift-fan inlet. In a mock-rescue demonstration, the rescue collar was inadvertently ingested into the left wing fan and the aircraft hit the ground at a moderate sink rate. Unfortunately, the trajectory of the ejection seat was unfavorable and the pilot was killed. The aircraft was extensively damaged, but it was rebuilt into the XV-5B configuration with several improvements for continued flight testing.

Ames flight tests of the XV-5 conducted in the period August 1968 to January 1971 involved a thorough study of flightpath control requirements in steep terminal-area approaches and for measuring noise footprints (fig. 90). It was noted that the handling qualities were unsatisfactory in hover and in low-speed flight because of low directional stability and low yaw control power. Short-field-landing characteristics were compromised by hot-gas ingestion, and large ram drag of the nose lift-fan limited takeoff acceleration performance.

Although plagued by demonstration problems, the XV-5 proved to be a valuable research tool, and the lift-fan propulsion system had few mechanical problems. It was relatively quiet and the low exhaust velocities allowed approaches to hover on the ramp next to building N-211. Follow-on lift-fan proposals were offered, but none was developed. Again, it appeared that the added weight, complexity, and loss of space for fuel offset any VTOL operational utility.

Once again, the Ames research aircraft was given to the Army museum in Ft. Rucker, Alabama.

Miscellaneous Aircraft Programs

An Unusual Wing Planform

Landing approach problems of aircraft designed for very high-speed flight were of special interest for flight research at Ames. Common to many aircraft tested was the fact that landing approach speeds were limited by the ability of the pilot to precisely control flightpath (primarily altitude) in the landing approach. Wind-tunnel tests indicated that some wing designs that were optimized for very high-speed flight might have favorable high-lift characteristics to permit low landing approach airspeeds. One of these, the reflexed Gothic or ogee shape with a sharp leading edge was tested on a Douglas F5D-1 Skylancer aircraft in September 1965 (fig. 91). Although not publicly disclosed, this particular planform shape was obtained from French engineers who designed the British/French supersonic Concorde transport.

This wing design induces the development of strong wing leading-edge vortices which favorably suppress boundary-layer flow separation and allow the wing to continue to develop lift at high angles of attack. Determining whether the vortex flow was unstable and might adversely influence aircraft dynamic stability was a matter of special interest in the flight program. The flow behavior was visualized by observing tuft patterns and water vapor condensation trails, which were visible for most atmospheric flight conditions (fig. 92).

The flight tests showed that the ogee shape resulted in improved lateral-directional control and allowed a 10-15 knot reduction in approach speed compared with that of the unmodified aircraft. Although the condensation vapor trails indicated a vortex bursting phenomenon at the highest angles of attack tested (24-30 degrees), the aircraft dynamic behavior was not adversely disturbed.

This program was another good example of the versatility of early flight research. The wing shape modification was constructed of wood and attached to the metal skin using glass fiber material. For safety, airspeeds were limited to 250 knots. The entire program took less than 6 months.

There was a return exposure to the ogee planform used on the Concorde SST (fig. 93) in September 1972 when an Ames pilot had an opportunity to fly the

The Douglas F5D-1 Skylancer.

Concorde in Toulouse, France. Prior exposure to the flight characteristics of the Concorde had taken place using the Ames Flight Simulator for Advanced Aircraft. Of particular interest in the Ames studies was an examination of performance requirements related to certification standards. Because of the possibility that performance data would be obtained that might adversely penalize operation of the Concorde, a cooperative program with French and British participation was arranged. The chief test pilots from both countries verified that the Concorde performance characteristics were correctly represented in the simulation, and that the simulation would not adversely influence operational evaluations.

Stability and control characteristics were evaluated in the flight program up to the cruise Mach number of 2.0 (540 knots indicated airspeed at 50,000 feet). Most of the flight time was used to investigate approach and landing, which in the simulator tests aroused special interest because of a pronounced nose-down pitch tendency when entering ground effect. A technique was developed to anticipate the requirement for a nose-up pitch-control input. The flight tests confirmed the accuracy of the ground-effect model used on the simulator, and the pilot noted that the final flare was controlled satisfactorily.

Although Ames participation in the development of this unique transport was not extensive, Ames' expertise helped establish confidence that this unusual concept, which is still operating today, would be safe to fly in routine operation at twice the speed of sound.

Comparison of Engine Air Inlets

Performance of jet-powered aircraft in the transonic speed range was an area of strong interest for Ames flight research. A program conducted on two North American YF-93 aircraft in the early 1950s compared the overall high-speed performance using two different inlet configurations: (1) a submerged divergent-wall inlet (fig. 94) and (2) a scoop inlet (fig. 95). Included in the study were the pressure-recovery characteristics of the inlets and the overall airplane drag for each configuration. The scope of the program covered tests in the Mach range from 0.50 to 1.05 by varying engine speeds from idle to full power, including operation with afterburner.

To achieve the desired results, engine thrust and aircraft airspeed had to be determined very accurately. Two points of interest were (1) the hardware and mechanism used for measuring engine thrust, and (2) the method used for calibrating the airspeed systems.

Engine thrust was obtained by measuring total pressure in the engine tailpipe by a "swinging" probe which traversed the exit area in a radial arc. Because exhaust temperatures were very high in afterburner mode (3,500 °F), a unique cooling system using compressor bleed air for the probe was devised.

For airspeed measurements, it became common practice at Ames to calibrate the airspeed system by using a flyby method in which the static pressure measured in the aircraft was compared with the barometric (static) pressure at ground level. An observer on the ground used a phototheodolite to obtain the actual altitude of the airplane above ground level. The aircraft was flown by the ground station at various airspeeds, up to the maximum obtainable (Mach 1.05). It may be of interest to note that because the aircraft was approaching the observer at airspeeds near the speed of sound (over 700 mph), no noise was perceived until the aircraft reached the observer. Then instantaneously, the sound generated by the aircraft pressure wave and engine exhaust arrived with the force of an explosion. This is an experience I still vividly recall.

The results of the tests indicated the following: (1) the submerged inlet had higher pressure recoveries throughout most of the Mach number range tested, but it also had higher drag than the scoop inlet below Mach 0.89, and (2) compared on the basis of a factor that combined the thrust differences and the drag differences, level flight speed was about the same, regardless of the type of inlet.

For whatever reasons, most jet aircraft over the years used a scoop inlet for the engine air and submerged inlets for cooling internal accessories.

Increased Lift with Boundary-Layer Control

Swept-wing aircraft designed for high-speed flight have higher landing approach speeds and require longer runways for operational use than their straight-wing counterparts. Ames large-scale wind-tunnel tests in the early 1950s indicated that the low-speed lift characteristics of swept-wing aircraft could be improved by using boundary-layer control (BLC) to reduce flow separation at both the leading and trailing edges of the wing. Questions remained regarding the realizability of the lift improvements in flight and any operational problems that might arise. Ames took a lead role in developing and flight testing advanced BLC systems and gained worldwide recognition as a leading authority in high-lift systems.

Two methods for improving lift were examined in Ames flight-research tests in the 1950s of several types of aircraft. One used suction through a porous material to remove low energy (stagnant) flow in the wing boundary layer, and the other, called blowing BLC, used a high-velocity air jet to reenergize the flow and delay separation. In the first study, suction was applied to an area near the leading edge of the trailing-edge flap and also along the entire span of the wing leading edge. In the blowing BLC study, high-velocity air from the engine compressor was ejected from the leading edge of the flap radius at both leading and trailing edges.

North American F-86—Two types of BLC—suction and blowing—were used to reduce boundary-layer flow separation on an F-86 swept-wing aircraft (fig. 96). Suction was obtained from an ejector pump system which used a diffuser to improve efficiency. The following points were of interest: (1) the magnitude of lift increments owing to suction or blowing, (2) the effect on the low-speed flying qualities and serviceability of the airplane, and (3) the manner in which the pilot made use of the lift increments provided by BLC.

The F-86 flight results showed that area suction allowed higher flap deflections with increased lift and a 6-knot reduction in approach speed. No detrimental effects attributable to BLC were noted. The blowing BLC provided larger lift gains, reducing landing approach speed by 12 knots. The leading-edge suction BLC system reduced stall speed by 22 knots with a 20-knot reduction in approach speed. This system was flown in rain with no performance loss with BLC.

In summary, evaluation flights by 16 pilots indicated several improvements when BLC was used. The blowing system produced larger lift gains, but with a larger reduction in engine static thrust because of bleed-air extraction from the compressor. The suction systems used about 10% less bleed air than the blowing systems, which provided improved takeoff performance but considerably less lift gains. In either case, pilots noted an improvement in approach flight-path control with BLC.

North American F-100A—To extend boundary-layer control studies to wings of greater sweep and reduced thickness ratio, tests were conducted on a modified F-100A (fig. 97) with blowing BLC on the trailing-edge flaps deflected 45 degrees and on leading-edge flaps (fig. 98) deflected 60 degrees. There are two points of interest regarding lift improvements: (1) the effect on the pilot's choice of approach speed, and (2) the amount of increased wing lift usable for low-speed operation by preventing wing leading-edge stall.

With BLC applied to the trailing-edge flaps, increases in flap lift increment of 100% were realized. Landing approach speeds were reduced by about 10 knots, and roll capability at 170 knots was increased 30%. Further reduction in approach speed was limited by pilot ability to control flight-path angle and to arrest sink rate. Another factor was a reduction in engine thrust available to maintain airspeed when maneuvering during low-speed flight. A modification to the engine inlet (fig. 99) was made to improve pressure recovery for test purposes.

Improvements obtained with BLC on the highly deflected leading-edge flap were equally impressive. Compared with the slatted leading edge, stall speed was reduced 9% and landing approach speed decreased 9%. Most important were better handling characteristics consisting of the elimination of objectionable wing buffet, improved stalling characteristics, and elimination of static longitudinal instability in the landing approach. An upper limit on usable angle of attack was apparent from three factors: (1) an adverse pitch change with thrust, (2) sideslip due to roll about the inclined pitch axis, and (3) low directional stability.

The North American F-100A Super Sabre.

Test pilot Commander L. Heyworth Jr., USN with Seth Anderson beside a North American FJ-3.

Leading-edge blowing BLC was incorporated on the F-100 aircraft for a short period, but discontinued because of extra maintenance costs.

Grumman F9F-4—Application of BLC to a Navy operational fighter was sponsored by the Bureau of Aeronautics in late 1956, and a Grumman F9F-4 was lent to Ames for flight evaluation. The aircraft (fig. 100) was modified to use a high-energy compressor bleed-air blowing system over the trailing-edge flap deflected 45 degrees.

Use of blowing BLC increased the maximum lift coefficient in the approach condition from 1.98 to 2.32, which resulted in a 10-knot reduction in approach speed. Takeoff distances showed little improvement with BLC, a result of the reduction in engine thrust associated with use of compressor bleed air.

Other aircraft deficiencies associated with lower-speed flight included poor stall characteristics (large roll-off, lack of stall warning), and poor lateral-directional stability, which was not improved with the BLC system.

The added weight and complexity of the BLC system apparently offset approach speed advantages and the Navy elected not to incorporate BLC modifications to this series of aircraft.

North American FJ-3—Another Navy aircraft designed for carrier operation and tested at Ames was the FJ-3 (fig. 101). This aircraft was similar to the Air Force F-86, but had a stronger (heavier) landing gear for carrier landings and catapult takeoff. The ability to achieve desired low-speed performance with added weight was an important safety concern. Previous Ames flight tests had shown that appreciable lift improvements were available by using BLC on trailing-edge flaps. Ames expertise in designing, constructing, and installing BLC systems was recognized worldwide.

In 1957, the Navy Bureau of Aeronautics asked NACA Ames to flight test two types of BLC systems on the FJ-3; one a suction system and the other a blowing system. The suction system used less engine bleed air and, therefore, more thrust was available for takeoff. In comparison, blowing resulted in larger lift gains but less engine thrust.

Ames and Navy pilots evaluated the stall and approach characteristics of the BLC-equipped FJ-3 with various wing leading-edge and trailing-edge flap configurations. Results showed that carrier-landing approach speeds were reduced by both systems; however, a greater reduction (about 10 knots) was available with the blowing flap.

Summary of BLC Use

Considerable Ames effort went into researching the relative merits of various types of BLC systems on several types of aircraft. Although appreciable lift gains could be realized, only a few operational military aircraft were equipped with high-lift systems. Blowing-type BLC was incorporated on the North American F-100 Super Sabre, the Lockheed F-104A Starfighter, the McDonnell Douglas Phantom II F4H carrier aircraft, and the French Naval version of the Chance-Vought F8U carrier aircraft.

Currently, there are no aircraft using BLC systems. For Naval aircraft the need was mitigated by the angle-deck aircraft carriers. For civil aircraft, application of this advanced BLC technology was not cost effective.

International Flight Research Programs

An important input was made to the history of Ames flight research by programs involving foreign aircraft. Flight tests conducted in the United States and abroad involved Canadian, British, French, Japanese, and German aircraft. In many cases the flight-research areas of interest were focused by Ames piloted simulation studies and large-scale wind-tunnel tests. In addition, justification for conducting flight tests stemmed from a need to obtain quantitative data on aircraft flying qualities as part of a NATO member nation requirement to develop handling-qualities specifications for military V/STOL aircraft.

Improving the Handling of a Japanese Seaplane

A unique Ames flight-research program involved a 1964 study of the handling qualities of a deflected-slipstream STOL seaplane (fig. 102). This aircraft had four propellers and boundary-layer control (BLC) on all control surfaces and on the trailing-edge flaps. This enabled the aircraft to fly at relatively low airspeeds to reduce structural loads when landing in high sea states. The aircraft, designated the UF-XS, was designed and built by the Shin Meiwa Company for the Japanese Maritime Self Defense Force to operate in a sea state corresponding to 10-foot waves—a very hostile environment. The first flight occurred in December 1962.

Because of its established expertise in STOL flight research, Ames was invited to participate in collaboration with the U.S. Navy in a flight-test program of this aircraft at Omura, Japan, in 1964. Of interest was a determination of performance and handling-qualities requirements for the UF-XS at approach speeds of the order of 50 knots.

Obtaining satisfactory STOL handling qualities when operating at high engine power, high lift coefficients, and low airspeeds had proved to be challenging. Preliminary testing by the Japanese indicated that the basic airframe suffered from deficiencies in the STOL speed regime including the following:

- Pitch static instability at high angle of attack
- Negative dihedral effect
- Strongly divergent (unstable) spiral stability
- Excessive aileron adverse yaw
- Inadequate lateral control power
- Strongly unstable longitudinal phugoid
- Unexpected change in side force in ground proximity
- Control problems with BLC failure
- Generally low control power about all axes.

The handling qualities of the UF-XS were studied first in the Ames six-degree-of-freedom piloted motion-based simulator to provide a preliminary evaluation of the seriousness of the deficiencies and to examine potential solutions. The tests indicated that automatic stabilization equipment (ASE), which provided attitude stabilization, increased damping in roll, and turn coordination, was necessary to improve handling qualities to a satisfactory level.

Although there were no water landings under conditions involving high seas, the touchdowns at lift coefficients in the 4 to 6 range corresponded to 45- to 50-knot airspeeds. The only unusual behavior was a (yaw) heading change just as the aircraft approached touchdown. This was caused by the pressure established on the engine nacelles by the slipstream from like-rotation propellers.

Flight tests also disclosed that in the event of an engine failure on takeoff it would be necessary to reduce power on the opposite outboard engine to maintain straight wings-level flight. This would result in a forced landing since available power would be inadequate for level flight.

Ames participation in this program identified the need for specific improvements in lateral/directional characteristics for future STOL seaplanes. Apparently, the added complication of BLC and added weight discouraged continued development of this idea.

A French Connection for STOL Aircraft

Initial contact with the French aircraft industry regarding STOL aircraft was made in Paris, in June 1960. An invitation had been extended by the chief engineer of the Breguet Aircraft Company to review specific details of my recent publication on handling-qualities criteria for V/STOL aircraft. This encounter was a personnel communication challenge because the meeting was conducted under the assumption that everyone knew French. The language barrier problem was alleviated to some extent for the French participants by the fact that my NASA report had been translated into French.

The next day a new appreciation for French audacity reminded me that the French in many ways are different from Americans. I was part of a small group flying from Paris in a conventional French military transport to inspect the Breguet 940 aircraft, a STOL prototype being tested at the company flight test center in Toulouse, France. This trip provided lasting memories for me because during the flight the pilot, a decorated French military captain, came back to the cabin to chat about questionable areas regarding roll-control requirements in landing approach for STOL aircraft. After several minutes I became a little uncomfortable and asked him who was flying the aircraft. He replied quite callously, "The autopilot."

Ames had already established an authoritative international reputation for defining handling-qualities specifications for STOL aircraft when a second contact was made with representatives of the French Breguet Aircraft Company in 1963. Breguet had demonstrated the feasibility of using highly deflected triple-slotted flaps, cross-shafting for interconnected propellers, a control stick instead of a wheel, and differential outboard propeller pitch control to obtain outstanding maneuverability and STOL performance. These features were incorporated into an assault transport, the 40,000-pound Breguet 941 (fig. 103), which had four 1,500-horsepower turboprop engines. The 941 achieved good STOL capability by having most of the wing immersed in the slipstream and by using highly deflected flaps (98 degrees). Because of a mutual interest in studying the operational problems, performance, and handling qualities of STOL airplanes, Ames researchers made arrangements to conduct a limited 10-hour flight-test program on the 941 aircraft at Centre d'Essais en Vol (French Flight Test Center) at Istres, France, in 1963 (fig. 104).

The Ames evaluation provided a quantitative assessment of the handling-qualities requirements which could be used as a guide for improvements in the basic 941 design and for future STOL transport aircraft. The Ames pilot found the airplane quite comfortable to fly at the low 50-knot airspeeds required for STOL operation.

A follow-on 20-hour flight program with the aircraft was conducted in Toulouse, France, in late 1966 to extend previous studies to specific tasks associated with terminal-area operations. The program included the following: (1) transition from cruise to approach speed; (2) VFR and IFR landing patterns; (3) airspeed and flight-path control for these tasks; (4) landing flare technique and method of control; and (5) takeoff and wave-off characteristics.

These tests indicated that both heading and flightpath control were considered marginal in the lower-altitude instrument-landing-system (ILS) approaches. These tests clarified the need to develop improved displays and height-control characteristics for satisfactory instrument-flight-rules (IFR) operation.

Ames flight personnel were involved also when the 941 aircraft was tested for STOL operational compatibility in FAA-sponsored flights at the Dulles International Airport in Washington, D.C., using a small portion of the parking (heliport) area for takeoff and landing. Although these 1965 tests demonstrated the operational feasibility of this STOL transport, for various reasons civil use of the design did not develop. One reason was the added weight and complexity of the interconnect system needed for safe low-speed operation. Another and most important point was setting up the infrastructure needed to integrate slower-speed STOL aircraft operation into the overall airline transportation system.

Ach du Lieber Senkrechtstarter (VTOL Transport)

The first Ames contact with the legendary Dornier Aircraft Company, which is famous for many unique contributions to aviation, including the 12-engine DO-X flying boat, occurred in June 1960. I had been invited to Dornier Werke, Friedrichshafen, Germany, former home of the Graf Zepplin dirigible, by Herr Sylvious Dornier to discuss handling-qualities requirements for STOL aircraft. The status of several models that were being developed for military missions were reviewed, and an opportunity was extended to visit the company's private flight-test facility at Oberphaffenhofen, Germany, where these advanced twin-engine STOL aircraft were being flight tested.

This turned out to be advantageous for several reasons. I was given the pleasure of flying their DO-27 four-place aircraft from Friedrichshafen to the flight test center in the company of the Chief of Flight Operations. Because of old wartime cross-country flying restrictions, routing of flights in Germany in 1960 was along specified corridors which in this case took me close to one of Germany's most famous tourist attractions, the Neuschwanstein Castle, the construction of which was begun in 1869 by King Ludwig II, the Mad King. This fortress, a formidable mass of cold, gray granite bristling with towers and pinnacles sheltered by wooded mountains and the clear waters of the Forgansee lake, was spectacular when seen close in from 500 feet above ground level in circling flight.

Dornier DO-X Flying Boat.

Aircraft of interest at the flight-test facility included the DO-28 tractor-propeller, twin-engine, double-slotted-flap vehicle and the DO-29, a twin-engine pusher with engine nacelles that deflected down 90 degrees. The engines used cross-shafting to improve low-speed flight performance and safety. Adding to the pleasure of the visit was the friendly nature of the Dornier personnel who at lunch time greeted me with the ubiquitous German expression "Malszeit," which translates to "Have a good time eating."

A fresh stimulus for VTOL aircraft development was highlighted later in 1970 by Ames flight research in Germany with the Dornier DO-31 (fig. 105), a 10-engine 50,000-pound jet transport which first flew in February 1967. Because funding constraints and lack of experienced flight-test engineering personnel had delayed flight-test progress, there was an opportunity for a collaborative effort with NASA and approval for U.S. participation was pursued. Because this was one of the first foreign flight programs contracted by Ames, it was scrutinized closely by the chief of NASA Headquarters Office of International Affairs, who initially questioned the need to spend money conducting research in a foreign country. He suggested trading information from our studies on zero-zero landings. After reviewing the poor status of the NASA instrument-landing research program, he agreed to a go-ahead. In the end it turned out that NASA obtained over 90% of the DO-31 flight-test data for $300,000—a small investment, considering that Germany spent $30 million to build the aircraft.

Gaining approval from the Germans on the legal and procurement parts of the contract was equally formidable. This was the first time the Dornier Company had contracted with the U.S. Government and thus had not been exposed to interpreting the many legal clauses common to all government contracts. In addition, problems arose because the German Director of Finance (an old gentleman whose prestige derived from over 40 years of service and who had sufficient power to veto the president of Dornier) apparently did not know the counterpart to "nein."

The DO-31 had a cruise speed of Mach 0.60 and was a unique technological achievement. It was a high-wing, mixed-propulsion, VTOL transport with two main engines (vectored lift-cruise) and eight lift engines (fig. 106). For operational simplicity, all eight lift engines could be started simultaneously and controlled by a single lever. The aircraft was superior to other VTOL research aircraft in that it was large enough to constitute a first-generation transport with a mixed propulsion system and had an advanced control and stabilization system. The controls and displays were duplicated to allow IFR operational testing.

A hover rig (fig. 107) simulating the DO-31 was mounted on a telescoping base. The rig could be detached and flown in free-flight sideward and forward to 40 knots and to altitudes of 300 feet. It was used to develop the cockpit architecture and operational techniques for managing 10 jet engines in startup and hover flight. It proved valuable in pilot training and in total systems checkout.

A simulator program using the Ames six-degree-of-freedom simulator preceded the flight program and was used to briefly investigate the performance, handling qualities, and operational techniques required for a large VTOL transport operating in the terminal area. Of special interest in the simulation tests was optimization of thrust modulation for roll control. The program was of sufficient interest to have the chief test pilot and the president of the Dornier Company visit Ames to participate. They also expedited development of a follow-on flight-research test phase for this concept.

An 11-hour flight-test program was conducted at the Dornier Oberphaffenhofen Flugplatz near Munich, Germany, by NASA, including Langley and Ames pilots and flight-test personnel. The tests concentrated on transition, approach, and vertical landing, and showed that the design provided a large usable performance envelope that enabled a broad range of IFR approaches to be made. The program was completed quite expeditiously in winter-snow conditions with no flight delays or mechanical problems. Needless to say, operation of 10 turbojet engines in vertical takeoff was extremely noisy, but the hot exhaust certainly eliminated any snow removal problems. Based on the favorable flight-test results and on the development status of the design at that time, it was predicted that commercial V/STOL transport aircraft could be ready for service in the early 1980s.

Of course, this did not happen and the question is why. Although commercial V/STOL aircraft offer the potential of providing more convenient and efficient city-center operation, the total system must be cost effective. Unfortunately, V/STOL aircraft are inherently more complex than conventional aircraft which is reflected in increased acquisition and operational costs. In addition, engine failure is a more difficult safety problem. Although modern control systems can furnish protection from attitude upsets caused by asymmetric engine failure, loss of vertical thrust in hover remains a serious problem. Providing auxiliary power from a spare engine would not be cost effective. A final point is that the V/STOL systems required for operation occupy structural volume of the aircraft that is normally needed for fuel storage.

More than 30 years have passed since the foregoing tests were conducted, and there is still no commercial use of any V/STOL design other than helicopters. The DO-31 found a measure of fame in its final resting place at the world's most prestigious science and technical museum, the Deutsches Museum in Munich, Germany, where the original Lilienthal glider and the Messerschmidt 262, the first jet fighter, also resides.

The challenge to develop a *practical* V/STOL transport remains.

My Closing Days of Flight Research

The End of an Era

This story of flight research at Ames covered an approximate period of 30-years—from the early 1940s to the early 1970s. The story is one of aerodynamics and its many derivative disciplines—stability and control, propulsion, handling qualities, and the operational aspects of flight.

Where to bring the story to a close was, of course, an arbitrary decision. Nonetheless, it seemed appropriate to end my narrative with one of the last large-scale flight research programs in which Ames played an important role. I chose something that was unique and special, the Dornier Company's DO-31 V/STOL, which was a significant and preliminarily successful attempt to develop aviation's first V/STOL jet transport.

Ending these memoirs in the 1970s does not mean that flight research at Ames ended at that time. It continued on, focused on a few select powered-lift ideas and with a gradual shift of research emphasis from conventional aircraft to rotorcraft of various designs. The change was not unexpected. The military was the primary force behind the earlier research priorities and that force had begun to fade in the early 1970s. Moreover, there was a redirection of emphasis toward the use of human performance modeling and away from the test pilot, and toward management of operations on the flight deck and away from the cockpit.

Collectively, these changes in the fundamental and traditional ways of solving flight-related problems have profoundly altered the requirements for flight research as I knew it. The possibility remains, however, that if some old problems remain intractable and if new and unexpected ones arise, flight research may once again be called into the solution.

A Picture Story of Early Ames Flight Research

The following photographs constitute a pictorial review of flight research programs conducted at Ames Research Center in which I participated. My experiences span the period from the creation of the Ames Aeronautical Laboratory by the National Advisory Committee for Aeronautics (NACA) in 1939 to the transition from NACA to the National Aeronautics and Space Administration (NASA) and the name change to Ames Research Center in 1958, and beyond to the present time.

These photographs have been accumulated over the years and, in many instances, are otherwise unavailable. Their inclusion here complements the main text, makes them accessible to a wide audience, and, for the interested reader, provides a review in pictures of what we did in those early and challenging years of flight research at Ames from which we learned so much about the problems of flight.

Figure 1. The site for Ames development was still a dream in the early 1930s when the USS Macon dirigible was docked on the mooring mast preparing to enter the south end of Hangar 1. The clear area in front of the hangar toward the bay would be the site for construction of the Ames Aeronautical Laboratory.

Ground handling of the 785-foot airship required large areas that were clear of obstacles at both ends of the hangar. The USS Macon had eight large 560-horsepower engines driving outside propellers and a top speed of 87 mph. It carried five Curtiss Sparrowhawk fighters which could be recovered in flight and stored internally. Bayshore highway was two lanes with sparse traffic, and cars crossed railroad tracks. (Feb. 1935) A91-0261-3

Figure 2. Aerial view looking east shows early construction of the first NACA Ames hangar (building N-210) near the north end of the USS Macon dirigible hangar and directly across from the Navy free-air balloon facility. The long straight road at the middle of the picture bordering the west side of the field is De France Avenue.

A storage tank for helium gas for lighter-than-air vehicles and a mooring mast are at the hangar south end. The metal top of the tank is free to move vertically thus maintaining a constant helium pressure regardless of the gas volume. Dirt runways used by Navy aircraft in the 1930s are visible beyond the top of Hangar 1. (May 1940) 07-320-1E

Figure 3. Looking west provides another perspective of Ames hangar construction. Bayshore highway (U.S. 101), wide open orchard land, and the city of Mountain View are near the top of the picture. A pile-driver for use in starting the first wind-tunnel construction is at mid-right.

A tower for air-traffic control was situated at each end of the large hangar. (May 1940) 06-320-1E

Figure 4. The flight research hangar (building N-210) was completed in September 1940. Rooms for offices are on the east side. The NACA logo on the hangar roof was for aerial recognition. Starting construction of the 7- by 10-foot and 16-foot wind tunnels is in the background. There were only a few cars on unimproved roads. (Oct. 1940) M-921

Figure 5. The apron and taxi way at the north end of building N-210 were added in 1941. Preliminary construction of the service utilities building is shown at the upper left. Navy housing is shown at the top with tennis courts close by. The small two-story structure with the penthouse top at mid-left was for Navy communications. AAL-1449

Figure 6. Two Vought Sikorsky OS2U-2 Kingfisher aircraft are parked on the south end of the Ames hangar. The NACA logo has been removed from the top of the hangar as a wartime security measure. The 40- by 80-foot wind-tunnel construction has started along with the administration building (N-200) at the far left. (July 1942) AAL-4226

Figure 7. A Curtiss C-46A-5 transport, a flying icing-studies laboratory, enters the north end of building N-210. Wide open spaces and the mooring mast for the ill-fated USS Macon dirigible are shown in the upper left. (Mar. 1943) AAL-4963

Figure 8. The O-47A aircraft, parked on the yet to be improved south hangar apron, is inspected through the baggage door in preparation for loading instruments. Note that rigid aircraft tow bars were a luxury. (Aug. 1942) M-831

Figure 9. The 26 personnel who constituted the Flight Research Branch in 1944 are shown here, some in Navy uniforms. AD88-0234-1.1

57

Figure 10. A Lockheed P-38F Lightning fighter is shown on the scales for a weight and balance check. In the background is a Bell P-39 Airacobra with an on-looking "busy" crew chief. A Bell P-63 Kingcobra, used in aileron flutter tests is in the foreground with the "car-type" cockpit door open. (Feb. 1945) A-7116

Windows in the doors and walls at the north end provided good interior lighting.

Figure 11. View looking south inside the hangar at night shows 10 aircraft. In the foreground is a four-engine Boeing XB-17F Flying Fortress and a Vought Sikorsky OS2U-2 Kingfisher. In the far background is a Curtiss C46A-5 Commando. In between is another OS2U-2, a North American B-25D Mitchell, a North American T-6, a Douglas A-20A Havoc, a Lockheed 12A, a North American O-47A, and a Fairchild F-24. (Apr. 1943) AAL-3984

Figure 12. A 1946 view from the top of the Macon hangar shows the completed second hangar (building N-211) for large aircraft. A sidewalk extends from the front of building N-210 to the aircraft apron (no road) on the east side of building N-210. A number of new wind-tunnel facilities have been added. A-15714

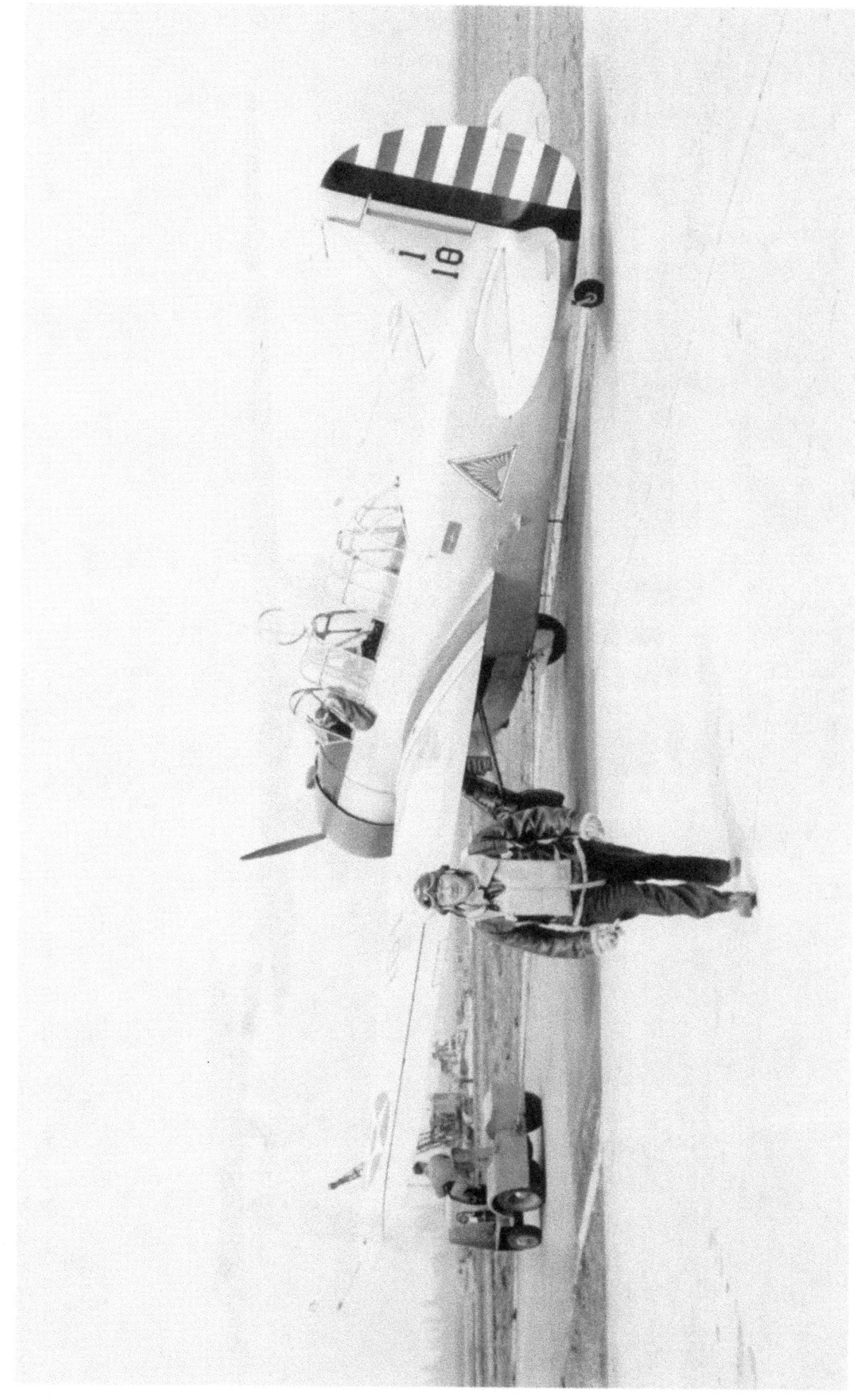

Figure 13. A new three-place North American O-47A observation airplane with Army Air Corps markings was the first aircraft to arrive at Ames. The circular antenna on top of the canopy is for direction finding.

A close look shows that help from the front cockpit was needed for directional control when using a rope (instead of a tow bar) to tow the aircraft. (Sept. 1940) M-925

Figure 14. A cable-braced vertical fin mounted at the mid-semispan of the O-47A wing was used in measuring parameters pertaining to ice accretion and removal. A heat exchanger system mounted in the engine exhaust provided hot air for anti-icing tests. This meager start was the first flight modification made to an Ames aircraft. (Sept. 1942) AAL-1436

Figure 15. The Lockheed 12A powered by Pratt & Whitney 450-horsepower engines. This aircraft was flown in very severe icing conditions after modification by the Lockheed Company to provide hot air deicing for the wings. An instrumented third vertical tail (barely visible in the photo) was added by Ames to study ice protection for this part of the aircraft.

A Vultee BT-13 basic trainer is flying in the background. (Jan. 1941) AAL-1166

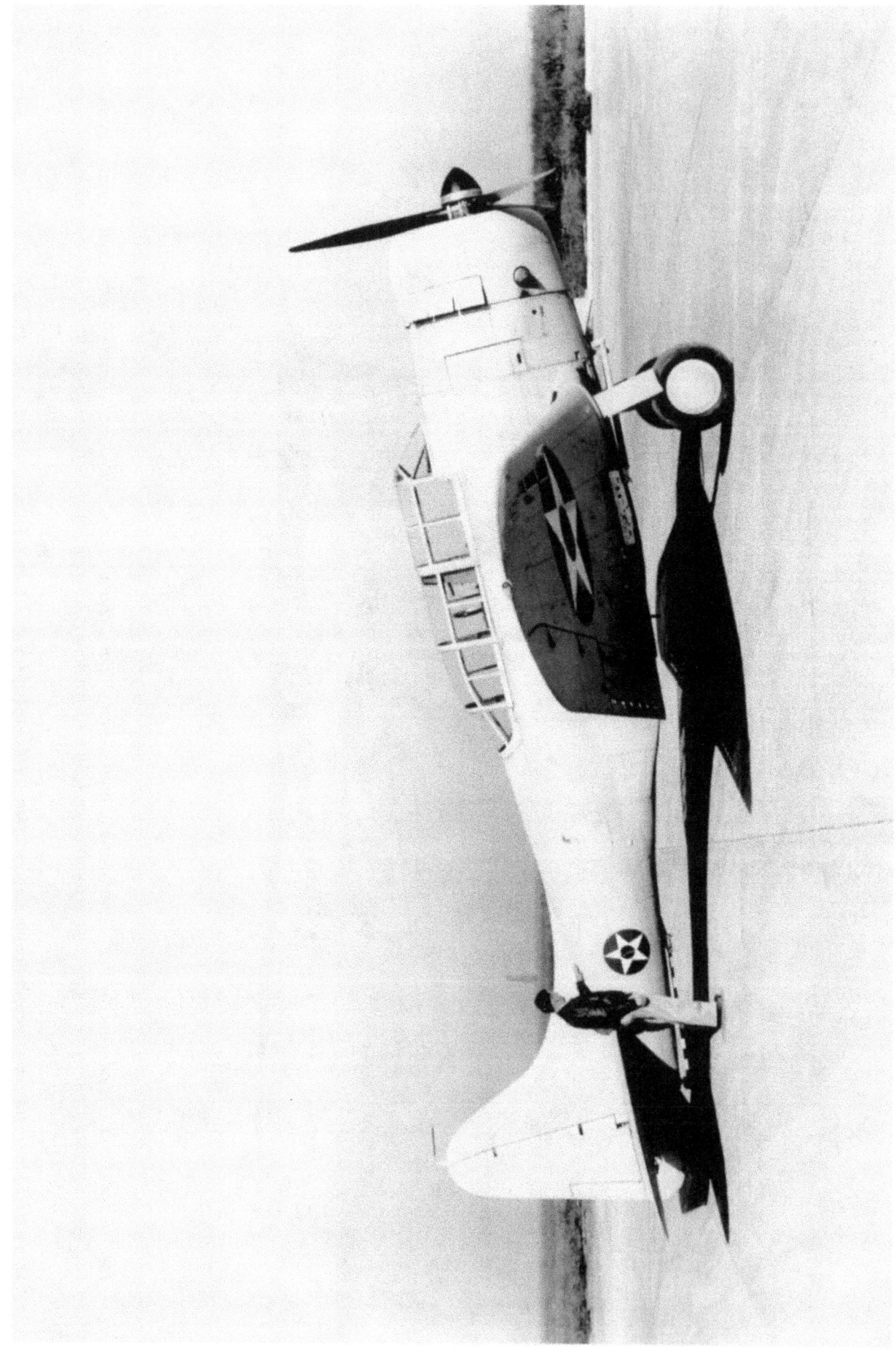

Figure 16. The Douglas SBD-1 Dauntless was the first aircraft used exclusively for handling-qualities research at Ames. This aircraft had low drag and was flown to 400 mph (0.70 Mach) in stability and control tests. (Oct. 1941) AAL-1646

Figure 17. North American P-51B-1-NA Mustang was used for a variety of flight research programs over a 4-year period. Its high-speed performance was superior to that of other P-51s, and it was a favorite among test pilots. (Aug. 1943) A-4931

Figure 18. The dorsal fin installed on the P-51 was one of several modifications tested in efforts to improve directional stability in maneuvering flight. This "fix" was retrofitted to all wartime models of the Mustang. (June 1944) AAL-5549

Figure 19. The Brewster F2A-3 Buffalo was used for limited performance and handling-qualities tests. Because of its high drag and low engine power, it had a poor combat record. Note the gunsight protruding through the windshield. AAL-2367

Figure 20. The Vultee BT-13 aircraft was modified following tests in the test-pilot's flight-test training program. Results showed that a dorsal fin was needed to improve directional stability at large sideslip angles. (Apr. 1944) AD00-0193-1

Figure 21. Vultee A-35A Vengeance equipped with research airspeed and yaw vane booms. Short engine exhaust stacks and fuselage proximity resulted in an extremely noisy cockpit with high concentrations of carbon monoxide. (Sept. 1943) AAL-4516

Figure 22. With dive brakes open, the A-35 could dive vertically without exceeding the 300 mph indicated airspeed limit. (Sept. 1943) AAL-4519

Figure 23. The North American P-51B-1-NA Mustang instrumented with sensitive accelerometers for making drag measurements. A tow cable was attached to the nose of the aircraft. Gliding flight tests were conducted with the aircraft towed by another and with the propeller removed. (Sept. 1944) AAL-4929

Figure 24. North American P-51B towed to an altitude of 28,000 feet by a Northrop P-61 Black Widow over Muroc Dry Lake, California. After the pilot released the tow cable, drag measurements were obtained at various airspeeds in a 20-minute unpowered flight. (Sept. 1944) A-6538

Figure 25. Lockheed YP-80 "secret" airplane pushed out from the south end of building N-210. It arrived in September 1944, and was instrumented in a secured "Blue Room." It was powered by a GE J-33 turbojet engine and was flown to Mach 0.866, a speed record for the time. (1946) A-6776

Figure 26. Lockheed P-80A fighter with instrumented nose boom. Scoops in the engine air inlet removed low-energy boundary-layer air to improve pressure recovery and engine thrust. (July 1946) A-10139

Figure 27. Measurements being taken to obtain the vertical center of gravity of the Lockheed P-80A by weighing the aircraft in nose-up and nose-down positions with the landing gear retracted. The cockpit canopy is missing. (Stairs leading to the second floor loft in building N-210 are in the background.) (Aug. 1947) A-11935

Figure 28. Martin B-26B-21 Marauder medium bomber with 6-foot extended wing tips. Entrance to the cockpit was through the bomb bay. Note machine gun protruding through the nose. (Sept. 1943) AAL-5506

Figure 29. Douglas A-20A Havoc attack bomber with flaps down. Note the unusual location of the airspeed probe on top of the vertical tail. The rear cockpit of the A-20 was equipped with flight and engine controls to provide emergency fly-home capability. Poor forward visibility from the rear cockpit limited flight-path control precision in landing. (Apr. 1943) AAL-3916

Figure 30. Douglas A-20A Havoc with yaw vane and airspeed swivel head installed on a fuselage nose boom. Flutter motion of the vanes could not be observed from the pilot's cockpit. A yaw vane is on top of the mast in front of the pilot's windshield. Cockpit entrance and egress were through the bomb bay. (Apr. 1943) AAL-3913

Figure 31. Douglas XSB2D-1 aircraft used in high-speed and takeoff performance tests. Gull-wing design resulted in a shorter, lighter landing gear. (July 1945) A-8290

Figure 32. Crash landing of a Douglas XSB2D-1 in an orchard in Sunnyvale, California (near Moffett Field), caused by engine failure. Note the spectator crawling into the rear cockpit to remove the clock. (Jan. 1946) A-9175

Figure 33. K-21 blimp seen through 40- by 80-foot wind-tunnel construction. Flight controls were modified to improve the K-21's handling qualities for long-duration blimp missions. (June 1943) A-FST-37

Figure 34. Boeing XB-17F with turbocharged engines. It was used in developing icing protection systems and for research on handling-qualities. (Dec. 1942) AAL-2497

Figure 35. The Boeing XB-17F was truly a flying fortress armed with 12 (and sometimes 13) caliber 0.50 machine guns fired from numerous gun turrets and a tail-gunner enclosure (Aug. 1942) AAL-2499

Figure 36. *North American B-25D Mitchell with research instrumentation used in handling-qualities studies. The B-25 carried a crew of five. (Mar. 1943) AAL-3919*

Figure 37. The Grumman FM-2, a popular, carrier-based Navy fighter, had good handling qualities. (June 1945) A-8229

Figure 38. General Motors P-75A fighter had counterrotating propellers. Two 3,000-horsepower Allison engines were located behind the cockpit; its performance and handling qualities were not impressive. The short exhaust stacks produced a pleasant melodious sound with the engines idling. (Mar. 1945) A-7414

Figure 39. Bell P-39 Causes of vertical tail failure in maneuvering flight of the P-39 Airacobra were investigated. An Allison liquid-cooled engine was located behind the pilot and connected to the propeller gearbox by a long driveshaft. This allowed for the installation of the 37-mm cannon shown extending through the propeller spinner. (Jan. 1943) AAL-4599

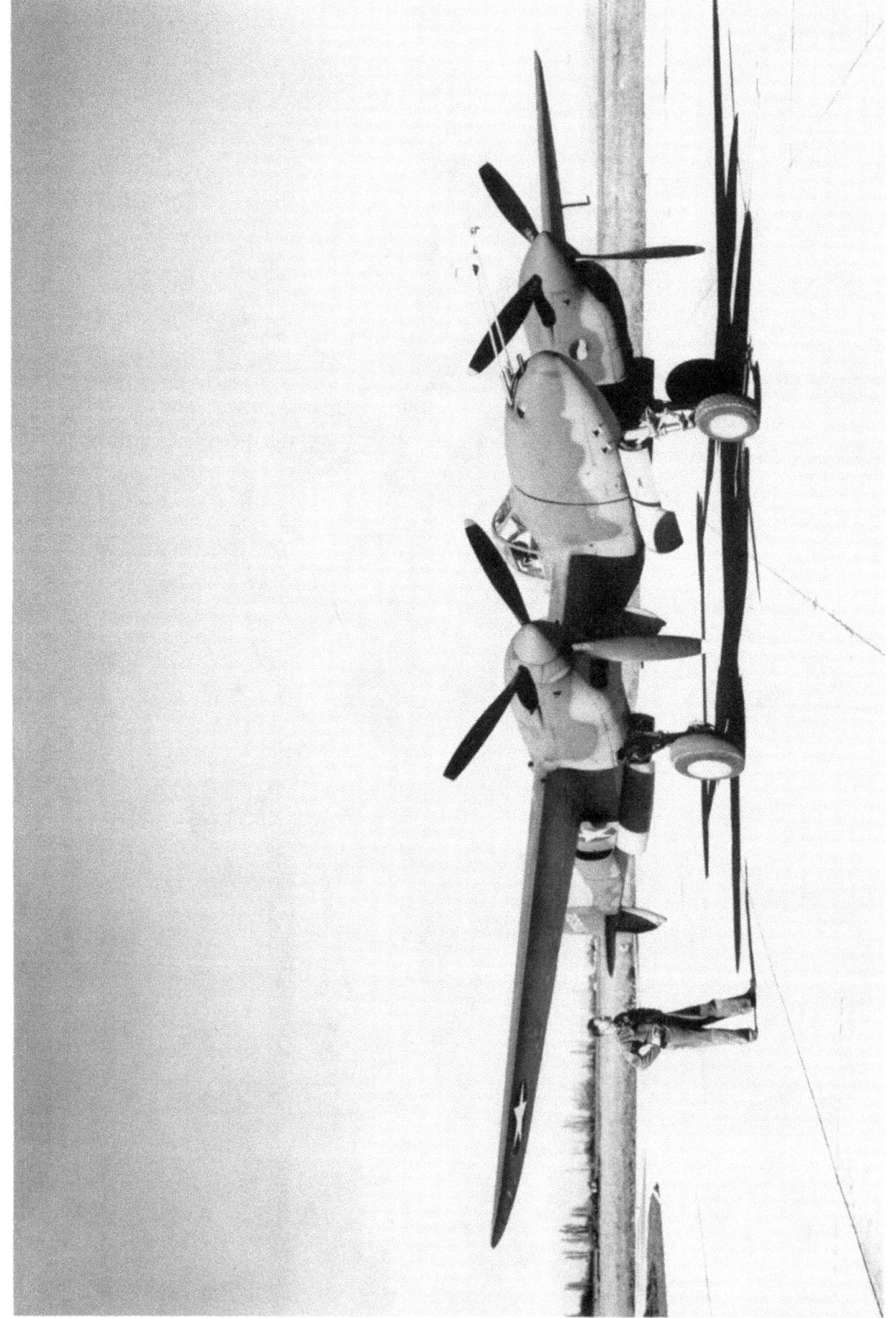

Figure 40. The Lockheed P-38J-15 Lightning shown with research instrumentation booms for use in handling-qualities tests. The free-swiveling airspeed head corrected flow misalignment caused by angle of attack and sideslip. The long booms tended to vibrate excessively at high airspeeds. (Aug. 1944) AAL-3507

Figure 41. This North American P-51H was used to test negative trailing-edge flap deflection as a means of improving pitch control in Mach 0.81 dives. A small reduction in diving tendency was noted. (June 1947) A-11703

Figure 42. Grumman F8F-1 Bearcat was used in tests of reflexed trailing-edge flaps. No improvement in pitch control was noted at transonic Mach numbers. (July 1947) A-11695

Figure 43. Flight test engineer checking Republic P-47M aircraft in preparation for handling-qualities tests and for use of the propeller for airspeed control in high-speed dives. (Mar. 1945) A-8444

Figure 44. Ryan FR-1 Fireball Navy carrier-based fighter with unique dual power plant consisting of a Wright 1,350-horsepower piston engine in the nose and a GE J-16 turbojet in the tail. (Feb. 1945) A-7222

Figure 45. Wind-tunnel tests showed that the lateral stability of the FR-1 Fireball could be improved by increasing the wing dihedral to some optimum degree. Shown here is the FR-1 with the largest dihedral tested—11.5 degrees. (May 1945) A-7959

Figure 46. Grumman F6F-1 Hellcat Navy carrier-based fighter modified to provide in-flight variable stability and control characteristics for studying lateral handling-qualities problems. (Dec. 1945) A-9110

Figure 47. The Lockheed P-80A had a strong diving tendency starting at Mach 0.78 (see fig. 48). (Oct. 1951) A-10141

Figure 48. The Republic P-84A had a climbing tendency starting at Mach 0.78 (see fig. 47) A-15464

Figure 49. The wing leading edge of F-86 fighter was modified by Ames sheet metal shop using mahogany. Greater camber and leading-edge radius increased lift coefficient; stalling characteristics were still unacceptable. (May 1957) A-22658

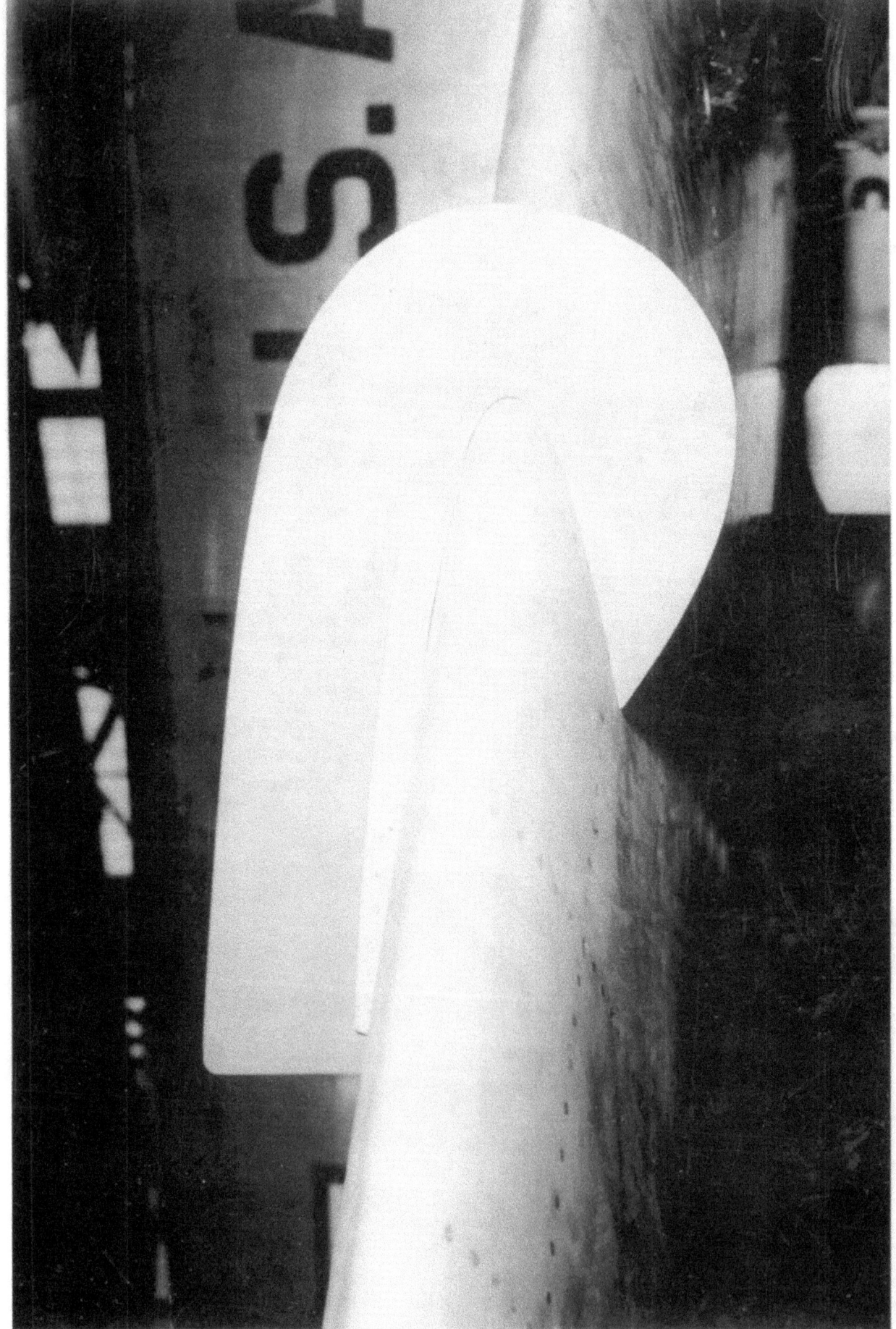

Figure 50. Short-chord fence was installed on the wing leading edge of an F-86A to reduce tendency for the outboard flow of the boundary layer in an effort to improve stall behavior. (May 1954) A-19282

Figure 51. Multiple fences on F-86A wing reduced flow separation outboard with less roll-off at stall. Additional fences strongly reduced wing maximum lift. (Nov. 1952) A-17733

Figure 52. Vortex generators on the forward chord of the F-86 wing reduced flow separation at high transonic Mach numbers. Note the Fairchild F-24 utility aircraft used for test pilot training in the background. (Feb. 1952) A-16086

Figure 53. The Lockheed XR60-1 Constitution, a large double-deck, 190-foot wingspan, four-engine transport designed to carry troops and cargo. Vertical tail loads were measured in maneuvering flight. (Dec. 1949) A-15100

Figure 54. The handling qualities of the Hiller Rotorcycle were evaluated. The Rotorcycle was a small, 500-pound, single-place helicopter. Tests indicated that the vehicle was unsafe because of low yaw-control capability to the right; the design also had poor crashworthiness. (Sept. 1963) A-31028

Figure 55. Vought-Sikorsky OS2U-2 Kingfisher single-engine Navy aircraft with flaps and spoilers deflected. The Kingfisher was powered by a 450-horsepower Pratt & Whitney engine; it was a versatile Navy observation aircraft, sometimes flown with floats. (Mar. 1942) AAL-2237

Figure 56. Ames-designed, double-hinged horizontal tail mounted on the OS2U-2 Kingfisher provided increased lift for maneuvering and landing (Vultee BT-13 in background). (Feb. 1945) A-7431

Figure 57. Douglas XBT2D-1 Skyraider, a Navy carrier-based aircraft, powered by a Wright R-3350 2,700-horsepower engine with research instrumentation. The aircraft had serious handling-qualities deficiencies, including lack of stall warning and large roll-off at stall. (June 1946) A-10034

Figure 58. Douglas XBT2D-1 Skyraider carrier-based aircraft with 2,000-pound torpedo attached. The Skyraider was a dive-bomber land-based airplane that was also carrier-based. This installation did not influence flying qualities. (July 1946) A-7985

Figure 59. Lockheed F-94C Starfire with Ames-designed, -built, and -flight-tested target-type thrust reverser deployed. Ground roll was reduced 50% by using full reverse thrust. (Feb. 1958) A-23663

Figure 60. The F-94C's rear fuselage was modified in the Ames sheet metal shop to accommodate installation of Ames-designed thrust reverser. Afterburner equipment used on the F-94C has been removed. (Aug. 1957) A-22727

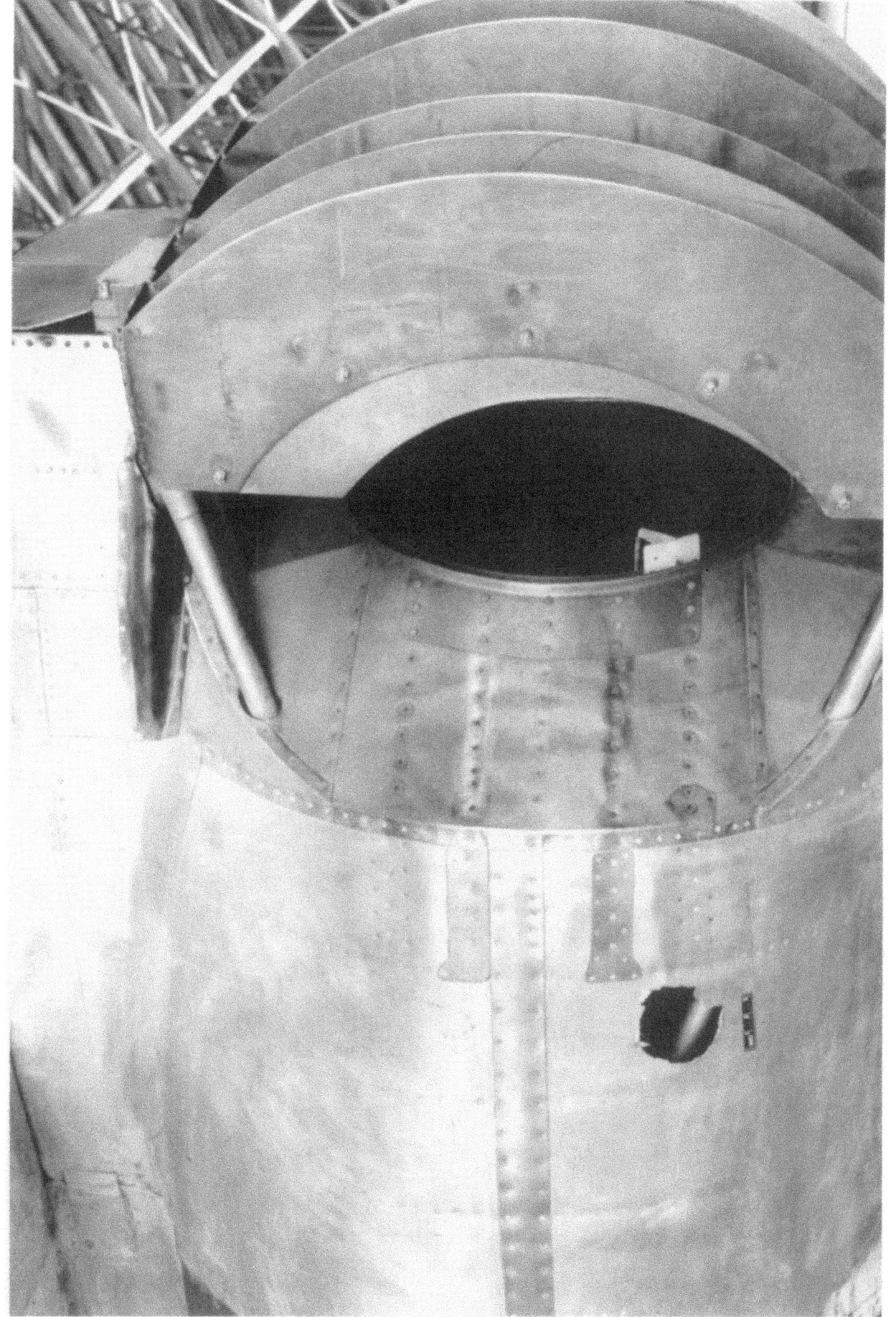

Figure 61. Close-up of damage to rear fuselage of F-94C Starfire caused by hot engine exhaust gases during prolonged use of thrust reverser in landing rollout. Fairing to cover rear portion of reverser has yet to be added. (Sept. 1957) A-23157

Figure 62. Close-up of target-type thrust reverser in forward thrust position (on F-94C Starfire). Titanium skin was added on the rear fuselage to withstand high-temperature environment. (1958) A-24153-2A

Figure 63. The thrust reverser on the F-94C Starfire was moved by an Ames-developed hydraulic actuator system. (1958) A-24153-1B

Figure 64. The Ames-designed thrust reverser for the F-94C received favorable publicity thanks to a nationally acclaimed radio commentator, Arthur Godfrey, who was an aviation enthusiast and supporter of NACA-developed technology. Also shown are the Ames public affairs representative and the chief test pilot. The Mona Lisa smile is part of the author's memoirs. (Sept. 1957) A-23316

Figure 65. Piper J-4 Cub with crosswind landing gear used in takeoff performance study. The flight-test engineer (the author) also throws the javelin. (Oct. 1948) A-13567

Figure 66. Piper J-4 Cub with the main wheels of the landing gear castered 25 degrees. This free-swiveling mechanism complicated operation in crosswinds on narrow taxiways. (Oct. 1948) A-13573

Figure 67. The Canadian built VZ-9AV (VTOL) "flying saucer" being inspected by government agents upon its arrival at Ames for evaluation. In retrospect, the VZ-9AV was obviously ahead of its time. Its promised performance (300 mph, 30,000 feet) was never achieved or even approached; indeed, it barely got off the ground. Ames testing disclosed serious deficiencies whose corrections lay outside state-of-the-art technology. (Dec. 1959) A-36413

Figure 68. A five-foot-diameter fan at the center of the VZ-9AV VTOL vehicle provided vertical lift and airflow to louvers and vanes at the periphery for thrust-vector attitude and translation control. The aircraft was not a success. An Ames test pilot called it a 3,000-horsepower siren. (Dec. 1959) A-36414

Figure 69. The eighteen-foot-diameter VZ-9AV VTOL vehicle mounted in the 40- by 80-foot wind tunnel at Ames for measurements of aerodynamic characteristics. At best, the cruise lift-to-drag ratio was about 4. Flight tests disclosed that dynamic instabilities prevented transition to conventional flight. (Jan. 1963) A-27748

Figure 70. YC-134A STOL aircraft built by Stroukoff Aircraft Corporation under U.S. Air Force contract with ailerons drooped and trailing-edge flaps deflected 60 degrees. An internally located J-30 turbojet with load compressor provided suction for boundary-layer control systems. Only a modest improvement in landing performance was realized with this system. (Mar. 1959) A-2073

Figure 71. Lockheed NC-130B STOL turboprop-powered aircraft with ailerons drooped 30 degrees. Note trailing-edge flaps deflected 90 degrees for increased lift. Two T-56 turboshaft engines, which drove wing-mounted load compressors for boundary-layer control, are mounted on outboard wing pods. Landing approach speed was reduced 30 knots with boundary-layer control. (Nov. 1962) A-28387

Figure 72. Nose-low pitch attitude of NC-130B was required in wave-off (or go-around) at 85 knots with flaps 70 degrees. An increase in stall-speed margin could be required to produce a more positive climb angle. (Nov. 1962) A-28248

Figure 73. Convair Model 48 STOL aircraft in landing approach at 55 knots. Landing gear was designed for no-flare landings (which greatly reduced landing distance) at 6-degree approach angles. This was a single-place twin-engine aircraft designed to Marine Corps specifications that required it to be small, simple, and inexpensive, and to be capable of single-engine operation (i.e., survivability). (June 1967) AAA-036-1.1

Figure 74. The Boeing 367-80 transport (707 prototype) was a large jet transport aircraft that had STOL capabilities; it had been modified by Boeing for these programs of two-segment noise-abatement approaches. Noise levels were reduced by 10 PNdB. (May 1965) A-37324

Figure 75. Boeing 367-80 STOL jet transport modified to provide shroud-type blowing boundary-layer control on flaps deflected 70 degrees. Approach speed was reduced 20 knots and direct lift control was provided by a slotted auxiliary flap. (June 1966) A-33973-1

Figure 76. The Bell X-14B single-place, open cockpit, twin-engine, jet-lift VTOL aircraft over Highway 101 in approach to Moffett Field, California. The X-14 was used by Ames to advance state-of-the-art jet-powered VTOL aircraft. (1980) AC74-4562-14

Figure 77. Bell X-14A twin-engine vectored-thrust VTOL vehicle hovering by building N-211 at Moffett Field. (Oct. 1964) A-28473-9

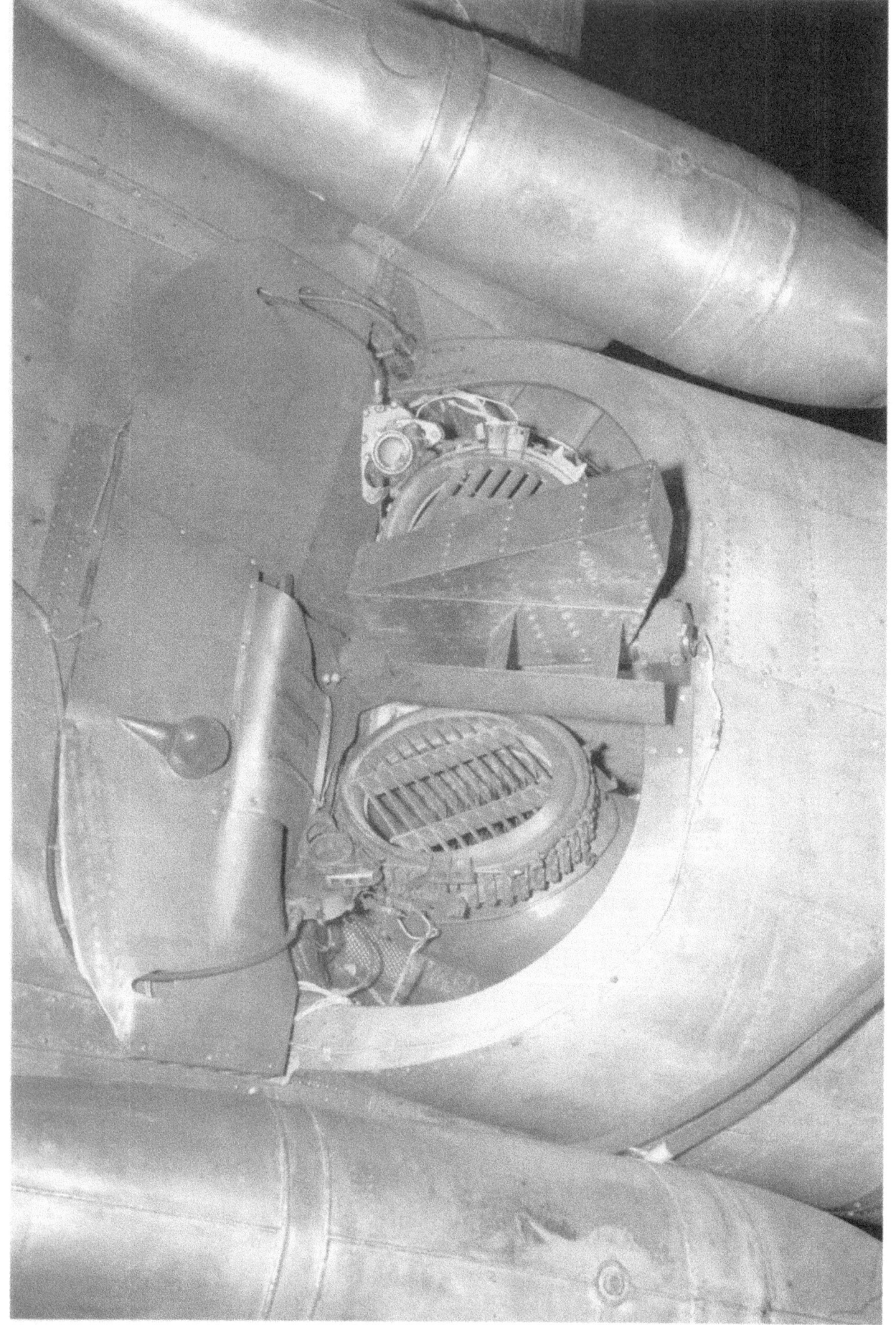

Figure 78. Cascade thrust diverters on the Bell X-14 VTOL aircraft could be rotated to deflect thrust vertically for hover or horizontally for forward cruise flight. (Jan. 1967) A-38766

Figure 79. Soil erosion caused by high velocity, hot jet exhaust from General Electric J-85 jet engines on the X-14 VTOL aircraft when hovering at 6 feet. In 5 seconds, large chunks of soil were hurled upward to heights of 8 to 10 feet, forming a crater 6 feet in diameter and 6 inches deep. (May 1963) A-30386

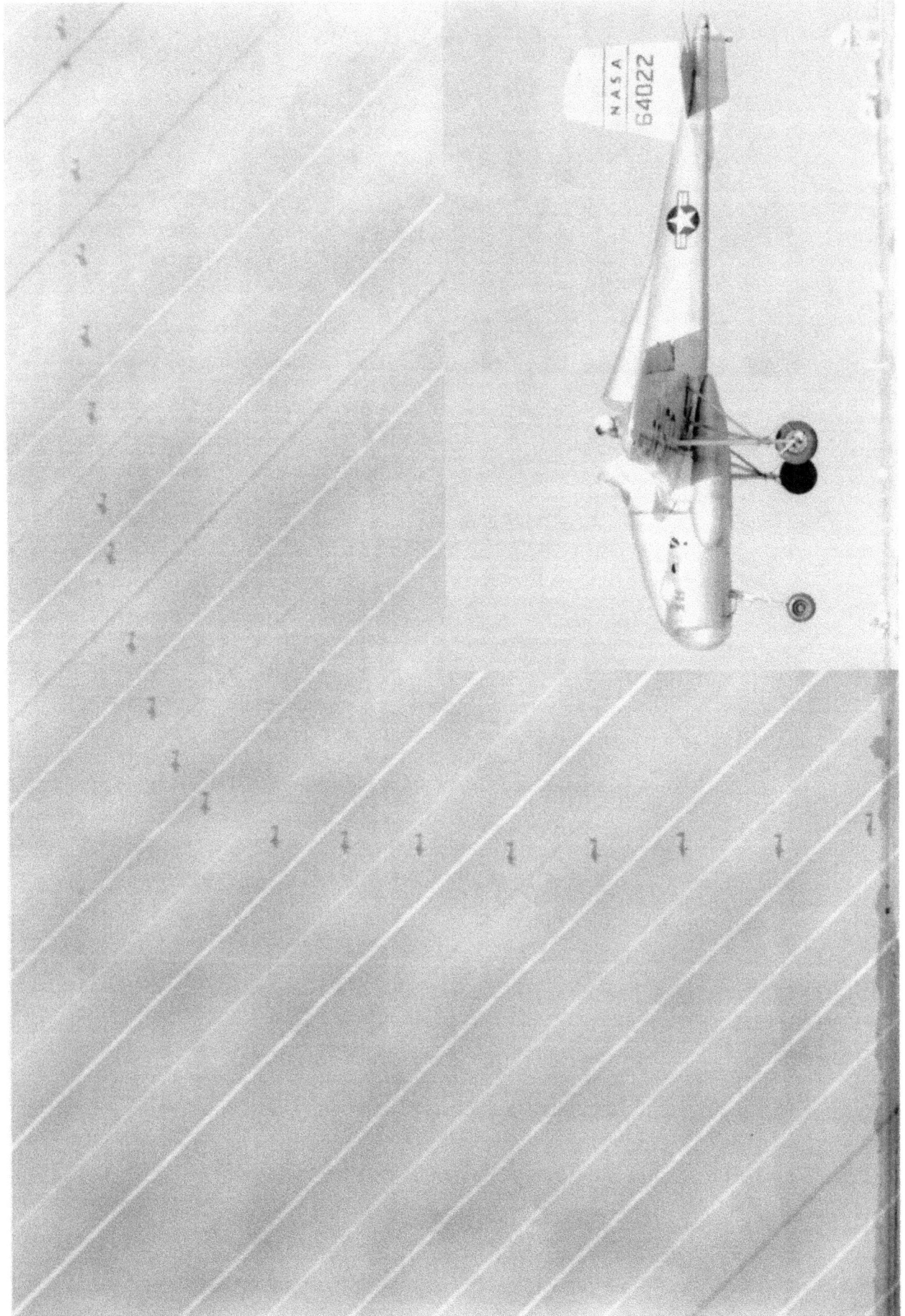

Figure 80. Bell X-14 aircraft in practice simulation of lunar landing trajectory flown by astronaut pilot. (Nov. 1962) A-29688-1

Figure 81. Ryan VZ-3RY turboprop deflected slipstream, open-cockpit V/STOL vehicle with large-chord highly deflected flaps. A single Lycoming T-53 turboshaft engine drove two counterrotating wooden propellers. The VZ-3RY design proved to be quite successful. (Jan 1960) A-30017

Figure 82. Ryan VZ-3RY aircraft over Ames in slow-speed flight. Smooth airflow over entire wing is indicated by tufts when wing had been modified to incorporate leading-edge slats. Tests showed that it could be flown at speeds as low as 6 knots when out of ground effect (which increases lift). (Apr. 1963) A-29657-1

Figure 83. Recirculation of propeller slipstream of Ryan VZ-3RY aircraft is indicated by smoke pattern. Recirculation caused a loss of lift and reduced lateral control at heights above the surface less than 15 feet and at airspeeds less than 20 knots. Engine exhaust vectored at rear of fuselage provided pitch and yaw control. (Apr. 1963) ACD00-0193-4

Figure 84. Bell XV-3 VTOL tilt-rotor aircraft hovering in front of building N-211 at Moffett Field. The XV-3 design combined a helicopter rotor and a wing. A 450-horsepower Pratt & Whitney piston engine drove the two rotors. The XV-3, first flown in 1955, was the first tilt rotor to achieve 100% tilting of rotors. The vehicle was underpowered, however, and could not hover out of ground effect. Note the large ventral fin, which was added to improve directional stability in cruise. (Oct. 1962) A-25685

Figure 85. The Bell XV-3 rotors tilted 45 degrees, halfway through transition from rotorcraft to conventional flight. There were no trim changes or flightpath control problems during transition. (Apr. 1961) A-26671

Figure 86. Bell XV-3 with rotors fully tilted for conventional cruise flight. Note large rotor-blade angle which reduced pitch and yaw static stability. Maximum cruise speed of the XV-3 was limited to 140 knots because of low damped lateral-directional oscillations. (Apr. 1961) A-26672

Figure 87. Ryan XV-5B fan-in-wing VTOL aircraft in hover at Moffett Field, California. The wing lift-fan doors are open and the nose-fan pitch-control doors are in operation. This two-place, 0.80-Mach research aircraft was powered by two GE J-85 jet engines and first flew July 1964. A-42628-11

Figure 88. This full-scale model of the Ryan XV-5 VTOL is shown mounted in the Ames 40- by 80-foot wind tunnel. The propulsive lift system was tested to determine power-on performance characteristics in preparation for flight tests. (Oct. 1962) A-32745

Figure 89. A full-scale model of the Ryan XV-5 VTOL mounted on an adjustable-height ground rig for power-on tests in ground effect. The nose-fan doors were modulated for pitch control. (Nov. 1962) A-32532

Figure 90. The Ryan XV-5B VTOL aircraft with widened main landing gear and low-speed control improvements for low-speed cruise flight. The horizontal tail was programmed to move 12 degrees in transition to powered-lift flight. (May 1969) A-42200-5

Figure 91. Douglas F5D Skylancer fighter modified with ogee wing planform designed for Mach 2 flight. Shown is the effect of vortex flow on wing tuft alignment in low-speed, high angle-of-attack flight. (Sept. 1965) A-33500-3

Figure 92. Modified Douglas F5D Skylancer in landing approach at Moffett Field. Vapor trails are generated by low pressure in vortex flow near wing leading edge on upper wing surface. Studies were undertaken in efforts to determine if there were adverse effects of vortex flow on the dynamic stability of the aircraft. A-33500-2

Figure 93. The Concorde supersonic transport with Air France logo taking off from Toulouse, France. The ogee wing planform was used on the Concorde to provide an efficient Mach 2 cruise speed. The cockpit nose is hydraulically drooped to improve crew visibility during downward view for takeoff and landing. AC88-0333-137

Figure 94. North American YF-93 with submerged divergent-wall engine-air inlet. Maximum high-speed capability of Mach 1.03 was obtained with afterburner on. Tests were conducted to compare high-speed performance of the YF-93 with different inlet configurations (see fig. 95). (Mar. 1953) A-16712

Figure 95. North American YF-93 with a more traditional-type scoop engine-air inlet (see fig. 94). Maximum high-speed capability was about the same for the submerged and scoop inlets when the afterburner was off. (Mar. 1953) A-16591

Figure 96. North American F-86A Sabre swept-wing aircraft used for low-speed tests of suction-type and blowing-type boundary-layer control systems. Several performance advantages were shown for both systems. (June 1955) A-20518

Figure 97. Blowing-type boundary-layer control on the leading- and trailing-edge flaps of North American's F-100A Super Sabre provided large reductions in takeoff and landing approach speeds. Approach speeds were reduced by about 10 knots. (Mar. 1960) A-24696

Figure 98. North American F-100 Super Sabre wing leading edge deflected 60 degrees for increased lift with boundary-layer control; takeoff performance was improved 10%. (Mar. 1960) A-24041

Figure 99. North American F-100 Super Sabre with rounded engine inlet; engine static thrust was increased by improving pressure recovery for better maneuvering in approach. (Mar. 1960) A-24039

Figure 100. A 10-knot reduction in the approach speed of the F9F-4 Cougar, a Navy fighter, was achieved by applying blowing boundary-layer control on the trailing-edge flap deflected 45 degrees. (Nov. 1955) A-20173

Figure 101. North American FJ-3 Fury swept-wing Navy carrier aircraft modified to test area suction- and blowing-type boundary-layer control on the trailing-edge flaps. A 10-knot reduction in carrier approach speed greatly improved the FJ-3's operational utility. (Sept. 1954) A-19681

Figure 102. *Japanese UF-XS STOL seaplane used blowing boundary-layer control applied to all control surfaces and trailing-edge flaps. Automatic stabilization equipment was required for low-speed flight. Operation in a sea state corresponding to 10-foot waves was possible with the boundary-layer control system. The special hull shape of the UF-XS reduced water spray pattern during takeoff and landing. (June 1965) A-33534*

Figure 103. Propellers on the French Breguet 941 are interconnected to provide engine-out safety and more efficient cruise with one engine out. The 941 had outstanding maneuverability and STOL performance. AD00-0193-2

Figure 104. French Breguet 941 four-engine deflected-slipstream STOL transport at Istres, France. Highly deflected triple-slotted flaps provided landing approach speeds of 55 knots. (Nov. 1963) A-31451

Figure 105. The Dornier DO-31, an experimental V/STOL transport, in forward flight. Four turbojet lift engines were mounted in each of two removable wing pods; they were modulated for roll control in hover and low-speed flight. Two vectored-thrust Pegasus main engines (15,000 pounds thrust each) provided Mach 0.6 cruise speed. (Dec. 1969) A-42712-2

Figure 106. Dornier DO-31 10-engine jet-lift V/STOL transport hovering at Oberphaffenhoven, Germany. Among other things, use of 10 turbojet engines eliminated runway snow-removal problems. (Mar. 1970) A70-3897

Figure 107. Hover rig mounted on a telescoping base was used to simulate operation of the Dornier DO-31 V/STOL aircraft. The rig could be detached and flown in free-flight to 40 knots for use in pilot and systems checkout. (Feb. 1967) A-38362

Glossary

Afterburner Device for augmenting the thrust of a jet engine.

Aileron Hinged section of the airplane's wing that provides roll control.

Angle of attack The angle between the wing's **chord line** and the free-stream velocity vector.

Aspect ratio A geometric parameter of a wing defined as the square of the wingspan divided by the planform area of the wing.

Boundary layer Thin layer of air near the airplane's surface where the air slows from flight speed to a rest, relative to the airplane. This layer is generally less than an inch thick on a typical wing, and is the source of skin fiction and aerodynamic drag.

Boundary-layer control A method of increasing the maximum lift coefficient by controlling the development of the boundary layer; for example, by supplying high-velocity air through a slot in the airfoil surface.

Camber The rise of the mean line of an airfoil section above a straight line joining the extremities of the mean line, usually expressed as the ratio of the height of the rise to the length of the straight line.

Center of gravity The point on the airplane through which the resultant of the gravitational force passes, regardless of the orientation of the airplane.

Chord (or chord line) A straight line connecting the leading and trailing edges of an airfoil. The chord of the airfoil is the length of the chord line.

Coefficient of lift Nondimensional value derived by dividing **lift** by the free-stream dynamic pressure and by the reference wing area.

Compressibility effects Changes in the properties of air flow as the flight speed approaches the speed of sound. This ultimately accounts for the formation of **shock waves** and a rapid increase in aerodynamic drag.

Dihedral The angle between an airplane's wing and a horizontal transverse line.

Drag A component of the total aerodynamic force generated by the flow of air around an airplane that acts along the direction of flight.

Elevator Hinged section of the rear of the **horizontal stabilizer** that provides pitch control.

Flameout Unintentional loss of a jet engine's thrust.

Flaps Hinged parts of the leading or trailing edge of a wing used to increase lift at reduced airspeeds (used primarily during takeoff and landing).

Flutter A self-excited vibration of the airplane's aerodynamic surfaces in which the external source of energy is the airstream and which depends on the elastic, inertial, and dissipative forces of the system in addition to the aerodynamic forces.

Ground effect Change in the airplane's aerodynamic forces and moments when in proximity to the ground.

Horizontal stabilizer Horizontal part of the tail assembly.

Lift A component of the total aerodynamic force generated by the flow of air around an airplane that acts perpendicular to the direction of flight.

Mach number Ratio of the speed of the airplane with respect to the surrounding air to the local speed of sound in air. Because the speed of sound varies with air density, the Mach number varies with altitude and temperature. Thus, Mach 1 represents a higher speed at sea level than at altitude.

Pitch Rotation of the airplane about its lateral axis (positive nose-up).

Pitot tube An open ended tube, usually mounted on an airplane's wing or nose so its opening is exposed to the relative wind. It acts to measure stagnation pressure for use in cockpit instruments (e.g., airspeed indicator).

Radian A unit of angular measurement. A radian is an angle which if placed at the center of a circle would intercept an arc equal to the radius in length (since the circumference of a circle contains 2p radians, 1 radian equals 360/2p degrees).

Roll Rotation of the airplane about its longitudinal axis (positive right wing-down).

Rudder Hinged section of the rear of the **vertical stabilizer** that provides yaw control.

Shock wave An abrupt change in aerodynamic properties (pressure, density, etc) as a result of airspeed locally in excess of the speed of sound, transitioning to a speed less than the speed of sound. Shock waves can occur even when the flight speed is less than the speed of sound, owing to local flow acceleration around aerodynamic surfaces (see **transonic**).

Sideslip angle Lateral angle between the airplane's longitudinal axis and the free-stream velocity vector.

Slat An auxiliary movable airfoil running along the leading edge of a wing. It is closed against the wing in normal flight, but can be deflected to form a **slot**.

Slot A narrow opening through an airplane's wing for air to flow to improve the wing's aerodynamic characteristics (e.g. delay flow separation). A **boundary-layer control** device.

Snap roll A rapid full revolution of the airplane about its longitudinal axis while maintaining level flight.

Spoilers Panels located on the wing's upper surface used to change lift, drag, or rolling moment.

Stall A condition of an airfoil in which an excessive angle of attack disrupts the airflow over the airfoil with an attendant loss of lift. It represents the maximum coefficient of lift.

Static stability Tendency of the airplane to return to and remain at its steady-state flight condition.

Thrust Force produced by the airplane's propulsive system; in conventional airplanes it acts along the longitudinal axis.

Tilt-rotor An aircraft equipped with rotors, the axes of which can be oriented vertically for helicopter-like operation and horizontally for conventional aircraft operation; the plane of rotation of the rotors can be continuously varied.

Tractor (airplane) An airplane having the propellers forward of the wing or fuselage.

Transonic The speed range between the high subsonic (~0.8 Mach) and low supersonic (~1.2 Mach) flight.

Trim tabs Relatively small auxiliary hinged control-surfaces on the ailerons, elevator, or rudder used to precisely balance the airplane in flight.

Vertical stabilizer Vertical part of the tail assembly.

Vortex A mass of air having a whirling or circular motion.

Vortex generators Small plates (actually, small wings) protruding perpendicularly from the wing that feed high-energy air into the **boundary layer** to prevent it from separating from the wing's surface.

Wind tunnel A facility that provides means for simulating the conditions of an airplane in flight by blowing a stream of air past a model of the airplane (or a part of it) or, in some larger tunnels, the full-scale airplane itself.

Yaw Rotation of the airplane about its vertical axis (positive nose-right).

Index

A-20, **59, 77, 78**
    airspeed accuracy problems, 13
    calibrating airspeed of, 12-13
    flying qualities evaluation, 13
    longitudinal stability tests, 13
A-35, **69**
    effectiveness of dive brakes on, 9, **70**
    flying-qualities deficiencies of, 9
Aerodynamic braking, 19-20
Aileron buzz, 10, 11
Airacobra. See P-39
Aircraft size effects on loads and response, 24-25, **101**
Air Materiel Command, 11
Airspeed accuracy checks, 12-13
Airspeed calibration, 10
Ames Aeronautical Laboratory, 2, 3
    change-over to Ames Research Center, 2
    flight research facilities, 5
    founding of, 1
    World War II influences on, 6
Ames flight research. See Flight research
Ames Research Center, creation of, 2
Anderson, Seth B., **40, 104, 112, 113**
    affiliation with Ames Aeronautical Laboratory, 3-4
    education of, 3
    first attempt at piloting, 4
    at Langley Aeronautical Laboratory, 3
    at United Airlines Cheyenne facility, 3

B-17, **16, 59, 82, 83**
    Ames modifications to, 15-16
    deicing modifications, 15
    in establishing handling-qualities criteria, 15-16
    pitch stability deficiencies, 16
    poor stall characteristics of, 16
    roll-control power inadequacies, 16
    with turbocharged engines, **82**
B-24, 5
B-25, **59, 84**
    elevator control power tests, 17
    flying qualities study of, 16-17
    in midair collision, 10-11
B-26, **76**
    engine-out flight tests, 11-12
Balloons, free-air, 25
Bearcat. See F8F-1
Bell P-39 Airacobra. See P-39
Bell P-63 Kingcobra. See P-63
Bell XS-1, 11
Bell X-14B VTOL. See X-14B
Bell XV-3 tilt rotor. See XV-3
Berry, Wallace, and Navy balloons, 25
Black Widow. See P-61
Blimp. See K-21 airship
Blowing-type boundary-layer control, 39-40
Boeing 367-80 STOL transport, 30-31, **122**
    bleed-air lift augmentation, 30, **123**
    noise-abatement analyses of, 30, **122**

Boeing 707, 26
    wing evaluations, 31
Boeing B-17 Flying Fortress. See B-17
Boundary-layer control, 23-24, 38-40
    on Boeing 367-80, 30-31, **122**
    in improving low-speed lift of swept wings, 38-39
    types of, 39
    on YC-134A, 29
Breguet Aircraft Company, 41, 42
Breguet 941 STOL, **151, 152**
    handling-qualities evaluation of, 41-42
Brewster F2A-3 Buffalo. See F2A-3
BT-13
    modifications to, 8, **68**
    stall tendencies of, 8
Buffalo. See F2A-3
Building N-200, **54**
Building N-210, 1, 3, **50, 52, 53, 54**

C-46, 5, **55, 59**
C-130 STOL transport, 29-30, **119, 120.** See also NC-130B
Center of gravity measurements, 11, **75**
Certification specifications for VSTOL aircraft, 2
COIN. See Convair Model 48
Commando. See C-46
Compressibility effects, 18-19
    on P-38, 18-19
Concorde SST, **141**
    performance characteristics, verification of, 37-38
Consolidated B-24 Liberator, 5
Constitution. See XR60-1
Convair Model 48 STOL, 30, **121**
Cougar. See F9F-4
Crosswind landing gear, evaluation of, 27, **113, 114**
Curtiss C-46 Commando. See C-46
Curtiss C-46A-5 transport. See C-46

Dauntless. See SBD-1
DC-8, 26
Deceleration on landing, 26-27
DeFrance, Smith J., 9, **9**
Direct lift control on Boeing 367-80, 30
Dirigible. See K-21 airship
Divergent-wall air inlet, 38, **142.** See also Engine air inlets
Dornier Aircraft Company, 42, 43, 44
DO-27 STOL, 42
DO-28 STOL, 43
DO-29 STOL, 43
DO-31 VTOL, 43-44, **153, 154**
    hover rig, 43, **155**
Douglas A-20 Havoc. See A-20
Douglas DC-8, 26
Douglas F5D Skylancer. See F5D-1
Douglas SBD-1 Dauntless. See SBD-1
Douglas XBT2D-1 Skyraider. See XBT2D-1
Douglas XSB2D-1. See XSB2D-1
DO-X Flying Boat, 42, **43**
Drag measurements on P-51, 9-10, **72**

159

Duct rumble, 10, 11

Eagle. See P-75
Edwards AFB, 9. See also Muroc Dry Lake
Electra. See Lockheed 12A Electra
Engine air inlets
    scoop, 38, **143**
    submerged divergent-wall, 38, **142**
Engine-out safety studies of B-26, 11-12, **76**

F2A-3, **67**
    poor performance of, 5, 8
F5D-1, 37
    in landing-approach flightpath control studies, 37, **140**
    ogee wing planform, 37, **139**
F6F-1, **94**
    as modified variable-stability vehicle, 21
F6F-3, **21**
F8F-1, **90**
    diving tendencies of, 19
F9F-4, **148**
    in boundary-layer control studies, 40
F-24, 8, **59, 100**
F-86, **23**
    in boundary-layer control studies, 39, **144**
    in flow-separation research, 22, **97, 98, 99**
    leading-edge modification, 22, **97**
    short-chord fence installation on, 22, **98, 99**
    as variable-stability test aircraft, 21
    in vortex generator experiments, 23-24, **100**
F-93 in engine air-inlet evaluations, 38
F-94, **26, 107**
    aerodynamic deficiency of, 26
    fuselage modification to, **108**
    hydraulic thrust reverser, **110, 111**
    thrust reverser damage to, **109**
    in thrust reverser development, 26-27, **107**
F-100, 26-27, **39**
    in boundary-layer control studies, 39-40, **145, 146, 147**
    with rounded engine inlet, **147**
    as variable-stability test vehicle, 21
F-104, 21, **21**
Fairchild F-24. See F-24
Fireball. See FR-1
Fisher P-75 Eagle. See P-75
FJ-3 in boundary-layer control studies, 40, **149**
Flight research
    in complementing wind-tunnel data, 2
    considerations of, in Ames site selection, 1
    defined, 2
    in establishing certification specifications, 2
    facilities, 5
    notable results of, 2
    objectives of, 1-2
    personnel at Ames, 5, **57**
Flight Research Building, 5, **52**
Flight test engineer, duties of, 5
Flight tests at Muroc Dry Lake, 9-11
Flow-separation control, 22
    studies of, 23-24

Flying Boat. See DO-X Flying Boat
Flying Fortress. See B-17
Flying-qualities evaluation of A-20, 13, **77, 78**
Flying saucer (VZ-9A), 27-28, 28, **115, 116, 117**. See also VZ-9A
FM-2, **85**
    flight-qualities tests, 17
French Breguet 941. See Breguet 941 STOL
FR-1, **92, 93**
    40- by 80-foot wind-tunnel tests of, 20
    lateral stability deficiencies, 20-21
    wing modifications, 20-21, **93**
Fury. See FJ-3

General Motors/Fisher P-75 Eagle. See P-75
Godfrey, Arthur, 27, **112**
Grumman F6F-1 Hellcat. See F6F-1
Grumman F8F-1 Bearcat. See F8F-1
Grumman F9F Cougar. See F9F-4
Grumman FM-2 Wildcat (VI). See FM-2

Handling qualities, specifications for, 2, 7
Handling-qualities research, 13, 14-15
Handling-qualities studies
    of SBD-1, 7
    of P-80, 11
Hangar construction at Ames, **50, 51**
Hangar 1, 12-13, **12, 49, 50**
Havoc. See A-20
Hellcat. See F6F-1
Hercules, 8
Heyworth, L., Jr., **40**
Hiller YRO-1 Rotorcycle. See YRO-1 Rotorcycle
Howard GH-3, 8
Hughes H-4 Hercules, 8

Icing studies, 6, 15
In-flight simulator, Ames development of, 2
Instruments, flight data recording, 5

Japanese seaplane. See UF-XS STOL

K-21 airship, **15, 81**
    Ames test program for, 14-15
    excessive column forces of, 15
    poor handling qualities of, 14
Kingcobra. See P-63
Kingfisher. See OS2U-2

Langley Aeronautical Laboratory, 3
Landing gear, crosswind, 27, **113, 114**
Leading-edge flaps, in flow separation control, 22
Leading-edge slats, in flow separation control, 22
Liberator, 5
Lightning. See P-38
Lindbergh, Charles A., role in Ames site selection, 1
Lockheed F-80 Shooting Star. See P-80; YP-80
Lockheed F-94 Starfire. See F-94
Lockheed NC-130B STOL. See NC-130B
Lockheed P-38 Lightning. See P-38

Lockheed 12-A Electra, 5, **59**
   in icing research, 6-7, **63**
Lockheed XR60-1 Constitution. See XR60-1
Lockheed YPO-80 Shooting Star. See YP-80, P-80
Longitudinal stability tests of A-20, 13

Marauder. See B-26
Martin B-26 Marauder. See B-26
Maxwell leading-edge slots, 25
Mitchell. See B-25
Moffett Field selection as site of Ames Aeronautical Laboratory, 1
Muroc Dry Lake
   flight tests at, 9-11
   P-51 flight tests at, 9-11
   P-80 flight tests at, 10-11
Mustang. See P-51

NACA site criteria for new laboratory, 1
National Advisory Committee for Aeronautics. See NACA
Naval Air Station at Moffett Field, 1
Navy carrier aircraft, improvements to, 20-21
NC-130B, **29, 119, 120.** See also C-130 STOL transport
North American B-25 Mitchell. See B-25
North American F-86 Sabre. See F-86
North American F-100 Super Sabre. See F-100
North American FJ-3 Fury. See FJ-3
North American O-47A. See O-47A
North American P-51 Mustang. See P-51
North American T-6 Texan. See T-6
North American YF-93. See YF-93
North Base, Muroc Army Air Field, **10**
Northrop P-61 Black Widow. See P-61
N-210. See Building N-210

O-47A, 4, 5, 8, **56, 59**
   in aircraft icing studies, 6, **61, 62**
   in airspeed calibration of P-80, 10
Ogee planform wing design
   on Concorde SST, 37-38, **141**
   on F5D-1, 37, **139**
OS2U-2, 5, **54, 59, 103**
   Ames-modified double-hinged horizontal tail for, 25, **104**
   handling-qualities studies, 25, **103**
   Maxwell leading-edge slats, 25
   pitch-control improvements on, 25

P-36, 1
P-38, 5, **58, 88**
   diving tendencies of, 18
   handling-qualities evaluation, 18-19
   high-speed deficiencies of, 18-19
   model tested in 16-foot high-speed wind tunnel, 19
   shock-wave-induced flow separation, 19
P-39, 5, **58, 87**
   aerodynamic loads measurements, 18
   vertical tail, structural failures of, 18
P-47, **91**
   handling-qualities evaluations, 19-20
   propeller used in speed control of, 19-20

P-51, 65, 89
   Ames modifications to, 7-8, **66**
   diving tendencies, 19, **71**
   with dorsal fin, **66**
   drag measurements of, 9-10, **71, 72**
   horizontal stabilizer failures on, 7
   in tow, **72**
P-61 in P-51 drag measurements, 9-10, **72**
P-63, 5, **58**
P-75, **86**
   handling-qualities evaluations, 17
   poor performance of, 17
P-80, **73, 74, 75, 95**
   center of gravity measurements of, 11, **75**
   as first U.S. jet fighter, 10
   flow separation in aileron buzz, 10-11
   handling-qualities tests of, 11, **74**
   instrumented for flight-test programs, 11, **74**
   in midair collision, 10-11
   pitch down tendencies, 22
   pre-production testing, 10-11
P-84, **96**
   pitch up tendencies, 22
P1127 Kestel (Harrier predecessor), 31
Piper J-4 Cub crosswind landing gear, 27, **113, 114**
Pitch control, 18-19
Pitch instability studies, 22

Republic P-47 Thunderbolt. See P-47
Republic P-84 Thunderjet. See P-84
Rodert, Lewis, Collier Trophy presentation to, **7**
Rotorcycle. See YRO-1 Rotorcycle
Ryan FR-1 Fireball. See FR-1
Ryan XV-5A VTOL. See XV-5
Ryan XV-5B VTOL. See XV-5
Ryan VZ-3RY V/STOL. See VZ-3RY

Sabre. See F-86
SBD-1, **64**
   handling-qualities studies of, 1, 7
Scoop engine air inlet, 38, **143**. See also Engine air inlets
Seaplane. See DO-X Flying Boat; UF-XS STOL
Shin Meiwa Company, 41. See also UF-XS STOL
Shock-wave-induced flow separation, 23-24
   in YP-80 aileron buzz, 11
Shooting Star. See P-80, YP-80
Short takeoff and landing aircraft. See STOL aircraft, VTOL aircraft
Simulator, in-flight, Ames development of, 2
16-foot high-speed wind tunnel in P-38 evaluations, 19
Size effects on loads and aircraft response, 24-25, **101**
Skylancer. See F5D-1
Skyraider. See XBT2D-1
Slats, leading-edge, 22
Slots, Maxwell leading-edge, 25
Sonic booms, 22-23
Spruce Goose (Howard Hughes' aircraft), 8
SST Concorde. See Concorde SST
Stall research, 22
Stall tests, 16

161

Stall warning criteria, 21
Starfire. See F-94
Static pressure measurements, 12-13
STOL aircraft, 29-35, 42-43
    Ames role in developing, 29
    Boeing 367-80, 30-31, **122, 123**
    C-130, 29-30, **119, 120**
    Convair Model 48, 30, **121**
    DO-27, 42
    DO-28, 43
    DO-29, 43
    X-14, 31-33, **32, 124, 125, 126, 128**
    YC-134, 29, **118**
STOL seaplane. See DO-X; UF-XS STOL
Stroukoff YC-134A STOL. See YC-134A STOL
Suction-type boundary-layer control, 39
Sunnyvale Naval Air Station, **1**
Super Sabre. See F-100

T-6, **59**
Texan. See T-6
Thrust reverser, 2
Thrust reverser development
    Ames role in, 26-27
    F-94 in, 26-27, **26, 107, 108, 109, 110, 111**
Thunderbolt. See P-47
Thunderjet. See P-84
Tilt rotor. See XV-3 tilt rotor
Truman, Harry, **7**

UF-XS STOL, 41, **150**

Valiant. See BT-13
Variable-stability aircraft
    development of, 21
    in lateral handling-qualities research, 21
Vengeance. See A-35
Vertical and short takeoff and landing aircraft. See V/STOL
Vertical takeoff and landing aircraft. See VTOL
Vortex generators
    on Boeing 777 transport, 24
    to control flow separation, 2
    in high-performance aircraft applications, 24
    in suppressing flow separation, 23-24, **100**
Vought-Sikorsky OS2U-2 Kingfisher. See OS2U-2
V/STOL aircraft, 33, 41-44
    certification specifications for, 2
    UF-XS, 41, **150**
    VZ-3RY, 33, **129, 130, 131**
    XV-5, 34-35, **135, 136, 137, 138**
VTOL aircraft. See also DO-31 VTOL
    DO-X flying boat, 42, **43**
    VZ-9AV, 27-28, **28, 115, 116, 117**
    X-14, 31-33, **32, 124, 125, 126, 128**
    XV-3, 33-34, **34, 132, 133, 134**
Vultee A-35 Vengeance. See A-35
Vultee BT-13. See BT-13
VZ-3RY, 33, **129, 130, 131**
    leading-edge slat tests, 33, **130**
    slipstream recirculation, 33, **131**

VZ-9AV, 27-28, **28, 115, 116, 117**
    disk-shaped VTOL, 27-28
    performance shortcomings, 27, 28
    propulsion system, 27
    wind-tunnel tests of, 28, **117**

Wildcat (VI). See FM-2
Wind tunnel
    Ames 16-Foot High-Speed, **19**
    40- by 80-Foot, **54**
        construction of, **81**
Wing fences in stall control, 22, **98, 99**
Wing thickness ratio in compressibility effects, 19
World War II influence on early Ames flight research, 2

X-14, 31-33, **32, 124, 125, 126, 127, 128**
    in pilot training for Moon landing, 32, **128**
    variable stability and control configuration of, 32-33
XBT2D-1, **105**
    control deficiencies, 25-26
    7- by 10-foot wind-tunnel model tests of, 25-26
    stall characteristics of, 26
    with 2,000-lb bomb, **106**
XB-24F, 5
XR60-1, in aircraft size effects studies, 24, **101**
XSB2D-1, **79**
    control deficiencies of, 13-14
    crash-landing of, 14, **14, 80**
    40- by- 80-foot wind-tunnel tests of, 14
XV-3 tilt rotor
    Ames evaluation of, 33-34, **34, 132, 133, 134**
    design shortcomings of, 34
XV-5
    fan-in-wing design, 34-35, **135**
    flightpath control studies of, 35, **138**
    ground-rig tests of, 34, **137**
    wind-tunnel tests of, 34, **136**

YC-134A STOL, **118**
    performance limitations of, 29
YF-93, 38, **142, 143**
YP-80, 10-11, **73**. See also P-80
YRO-1 Rotorcycle, 24-25, **24, 102**
    control limitations of, 24-25

Zap flap system on OS2U-2, 25

About the Auhor

The author with a model of an early Bede BD-5 aircraft, an airplane that he constructed and flight-tested.

Seth B. Anderson had a remarkable career in aviation research and development. With an MSE degree in aeronautics from Purdue University he began his work more than 50 years ago at Moffett Field, California, with The National Aeronautics Advisory Committee (NACA) and continued on with its successor, the National Aeronautics and Space Administration (NASA). His experience as flight-test engineer reached back over most of the modern period during which flight technology and flight research produced the historic breakthroughs and performance enhancements that characterized and propelled aviation's incredible advances. He worked as researcher and supervisor in many of the aeronautical disciplines, including flight performance, flight dynamics, and flight operational techniques as they relate to aircraft types that range from fighters and bombers to supersonic transports and vertical- and short-takeoff vehicles. He wrote more than a hundred technical papers and reports, held a commercial pilot's license and a U.S. Hang Glider Association Advanced Pilot Rating, was a Fellow of the American Institute of Aeronautics and Astronautics, a member of Pi Tau Sigma, a mechanical engineering honorary society, a member of Sigma Delta Psi, a national athletic honorary society, and a member of Sigma Gamma Tau, a national honor society in aerospace engineering. He constructed and flight-tested an experimental Bede BD-5 aircraft that was modified to accommodate a turbine engine. Seth passed away on April 3, 2001.

Monographs in Aerospace History

Launius, Roger D. and Aaron K. Gillette, compilers. *Toward a History of the Space Shuttle: An Annotated Bibliography.* Monograph in Aerospace History, No. 1, 1992. Out of print.

Launius, Roger D., and J.D. Hunley, compilers. *An Annotated Bibliography of the Apollo Program.* Monograph in Aerospace History No. 2, 1994.

Launius, Roger D. *Apollo: A Retrospective Analysis.* Monograph in Aerospace History, No. 3, 1994.

Hansen, James R. *Enchanted Rendezvous: John C. Houbolt and the Genesis of the Lunar-Orbit Rendezvous Concept.* Monograph in Aerospace History, No. 4, 1995.

Gorn, Michael H. *Hugh L. Dryden's Career in Aviation and Space.* Monograph in Aerospace History, No. 5, 1996.

Powers, Sheryll Goecke. *Women in Flight Research at NASA Dryden Flight Research Center from 1946 to 1995.* Monograph in Aerospace History, No. 6, 1997.

Portree, David S.F. and Robert C. Trevino. *Walking to Olympus: An EVA Chronology.* Monograph in Aerospace History, No. 7, 1997.

Logsdon, John M., moderator. *Legislative Origins of the National Aeronautics and Space Act of 1958: Proceedings of an Oral History Workshop.* Monograph in Aerospace History, No. 8, 1998.

Rumerman, Judy A., compiler. *U.S. Human Spaceflight, A Record of Achievement 1961–1998.* Monograph in Aerospace History, No. 9, 1998.

Portree, David S. F. *NASA's Origins and the Dawn of the Space Age.* Monograph in Aerospace History, No. 10, 1998.

Logsdon, John M. *Together in Orbit: The Origins of International Cooperation in the Space Station.* Monograph in Aerospace History, No. 11, 1998.

Phillips, W. Hewitt. *Journey in Aeronautical Research: A Career at NASA Langley Research Center.* Monograph in Aerospace History, No. 12, 1998.

Braslow, Albert L. *A History of Suction-Type Laminar-Flow Control with Emphasis on Flight Research.* Monograph in Aerospace History, No. 13, 1999.

Logsdon, John M., moderator. *Managing the Moon Program: Lessons Learned Fom Apollo.* Monograph in Aerospace History, No. 14, 1999.

Perminov, V.G. *The Difficult Road to Mars: A Brief History of Mars Exploration in the Soviet Union.* Monograph in Aerospace History, No. 15, 1999.

Tucker, Tom. *Touchdown: The Development of Propulsion Controlled Aircraft at NASA Dryden.* Monograph in Aerospace History, No. 16, 1999.

Maisel, Martin, Giulanetti, Demo J., and Dugan, Daniel C. *The History of the XV-15 Tilt Rotor Research Aircraft: From Concept to Flight.* Monograph in Aerospace History, No. 17 (NASA SP-2000-4517, 2000).

Jenkins, Dennis R. *Hypersonics Before the Shuttle: A Concise History of the X-15 Research Airplane.* is Monograph in Aerospace History, No. 18 (NASA SP-2000-4518, 2000).

Chambers, Joseph R. *Partners in Freedom: Contributions of the Langley Research Center to U.S. Military Aircraft of the 1990s.* Monograph in Aerospace History, No. 19 (NASA SP-2000-4519, 2000).

Waltman, Gene L. *Black Magic and Gremlins: Analog Flight Simulations at NASA's Flight Research Center.* Monograph in Aerospace History, No. 20 (NASA SP-2000-4520, 2000).

Portree, David S.F. *Humans to Mars: Fifty Years of Mission Planning, 1950-2000.* Monograph in Aerospace History, No. 21, 2001 (NASA SP-2001-4521).

Thompson, Milton O. with J.D. Hunley. *Flight Research: Problems Encountered and What they Should Teach Us*. Monograph in Aerospace History, No. 22 (NASA SP-2001-4522, 2001).

Tucker, Tom. *The Eclipse Project*. Monograph in Aerospace History, No. 23 (NASA SP-2001-4523, 2001).

Siddiqi, Asif A. *Deep Space Chronicle: Robotic Exploration Missions to the Planets*. Monograph in Aerospace History, No. 24 (NASA SP-2002-4524, 2002).

Merlin, Peter W. *Mach 3+: NASA/USAF YF-12 Flight Research, 1969-1979*. (NASA SP-2001-4525, 2001).

www.ingramcontent.com/pod-product-compliance
Lightning Source LLC
Chambersburg PA
CBHW080545170426
43195CB00016B/2683